D1525122

BIG Lessons
from
BIG Brands
Big Business Secrets You Can Use

Andrew Lock

AddictiveProductions.com LLC
Sandy, UT

BIG Lessons from BIG Brands

ISBN: 0-9777441-4-0
Printed in the U.S.A.

AddictiveProductions.com LLC
63 East 11400 South #255
Sandy UT 84070

Watch The #1 Marketing TV Show Online

Please accept my invitation to enjoy and benefit from my entertaining Web TV show, *"Help My Business!"* It's a 10-15 minute weekly show that's designed to help you build a better business. It's free, it's fun, and you'll learn a lot to help you move your business forward faster. Visit:

www.HelpMyBusiness.com

What Others Say...

"If you want to grow your business, make more money,
and beat your competition, read this book!"
- Ed Gerety, www.EdGerety.com

"Andrew has the unique ability to explain what large corporations are
doing in their marketing systems that are both beneficial to duplicate
or should be avoided at all cost. Learning and applying what large
successful companies do to help small companies grow their businesses
is one of Andrews's best skills. If you want to get the benefit of million
dollar ad budgets without spending like a mega corporation then you
should read this book and follow Andrew's advice."
- Bryce Anderson

"This book is full of great ideas that I applied to my own business
immediately, and I loved how its written in bite-size chunks,
perfect for my short attention span! Some might think that your
lessons wouldn't be suited to my massage chair business, but as I
pondered each chapter and idea, I found that I could use almost
every one of them. Thanks for these fantastic lessons!
- Dr Alan Weidner www.Massage-Chair-Relief.com

"This book is a must-read for the small business owner who wants
fresh ways to attract clients, but lacks a huge marketing budget and
staff of minions to do your marketing for you. Andrew is a
marketing genius who comes to the rescue by connecting the dots,
with easy to implement and low cost ideas. Bravo!"
- Carolyn Herfurth, www.TheBizTruth.com

"Read this book before your competitors do!"
- Isabelle Mercier, www.LeapZoneStrategies.com

The author, Andrew Lock, is available for a limited number of speaking engagements and about any aspect of growing a small business.

For information, visit:
www.AndrewLock.com

Contents

Introduction

Thank you for purchasing this book! It's absolutely packed with powerful marketing lessons that can dramatically improve the profits of any business. I'm very proud to present such a practical book. This is not marketing theory, I'm giving you proven methods you can adapt for *any* business.

Each chapter is based on the popular segment *"Big Lessons from Big Brands"* from my long-running WebTV show, *"Help My Business!"* If you haven't watched it, I invite you to visit **www.HelpMyBusiness.com**. You can also subscribe on **iTunes** (subscribing downloads each new episode automatically to your computer or device), by going to: **www.GetHMB.com,** and I'd really appreciate it if you would leave a review on iTunes, too.

I encourage you to read each chapter with an open mind. Although most of the examples wont be from your industry, the real magic happens when you think "how can I ADAPT this concept for MY business?" There's nearly always a nifty way to do that. If you consistently follow that thought process, within a few chapters you'll find yourself automatically thinking along those lines. Without further ado, let's get to the good stuff...

Andrew Lock

Chapter 1

Disney

Disney is a very smart company that thinks through their marketing and promotion strategies very carefully. This lesson is about the way they present their pricing for theme park tickets at Walt Disney World in Florida.

Take a look at this chart, below. What you see here is a reflection of what you'll also see at the ticket booth:

8

First, notice the headline, it conditions us for what we're about to consider:

"The more you play, the less you pay, per day"

Very clever - it has a positive connotation despite referencing the topic of price.

Then we see the sub-heading:

"$30 plus tax per day with a 7 day 'Magic Your Way' base ticket."

This immediately confronts (and destroys) the widespread belief that visiting a Disney theme park will be a wallet-busting experience.

Next, notice how the **most expensive** pricing options are stated first, at the *top* of the chart. It doesn't start with the one-day price, it starts with the seven day price, and they've even helpfully circled the top price to draw our attention to it. The obvious question is, why would they do that? Surely it would better to "hide" the higher prices at the bottom? Conventional marketers might think so, but remember that Disney are masters at marketing, so there's a lot more to this, based on what they know of human psychology.

Arranging the pricing in this way nicely accomplishes two important things. By drawing our attention to the premium price option first, it's made to seem like the ***default*** option that most people choose. In other words, knowing that people read from left to right, top to bottom, the placement of the most expensive ticket option forces the visitor to subconsciously *consider* the premium price option first as the 'default' choice. It subconsciously says, "here's what most people choose." If Disney were to bury the premium option down at the bottom of the list, fewer people would consider it, because it would be seen as a less popular choice. Interesting, isn't it?

There's another benefit to stating the most expensive option *first*. The natural comparison between the first high price option and the one day ticket price makes the one day look like a bargain. If someone knows that they can only spend one day in the park, they'll feel better about the price because of the comparison with the larger number!

I'll explain this further, because there's some interesting psychology behind it.

When you compare a large number with a small number, stating the large number first makes the smaller number seem smaller.

Look at this example:

$45,329.00

$97

The actual numbers are irrelevant, it's simply the fact that you compare a large number with a small number that introduces the effect of making the smaller number feel smaller. So in this case, when you see these two numbers together, the $97 amount subconsciously feels less than if you'd just seen the $97 on its own. Can you get your head around that? It's odd, isn't it?

So if a sales or marketing brochure features or starts with a price of $67, that amount would seem higher than if they had *started* with a high price and worked down to the lower price options.

10

And so back to the example from Disney, as you scan the price column, the amount starts high, and gets lower and lower as you get down to the one day option.

How to Use This Lesson In Your Business

Consider adjusting your pricing to present your *premium* priced product or service *first*. It will appear to be the default option, the one that most people go for. As a result, many more people will choose it, because it seems to be the 'standard' choice. It will also make your lower price offerings seem better value, in context.

Remember, people generally follow the crowd in making decisions. When presented with options, they naturally look for clues to guide them about which option to select.

This is very smart marketing by Disney, and sadly most small business owners will probably overlook this gem when glancing at their pricing brochure.

When reading marketing materials from a consistently successful company, always ask yourself 'why are they presenting the information in this way?" See if you can see patterns or clues that you can model.

Chapter 2

Starbucks

Hmmm, don't you just love a $6 cup of coffee? Whether you love 'em or hate 'em, Starbucks has managed to dominate an industry that revolves around one of the most basic, commodity products - coffee! How did they do it? Well, they do a lot of things differently from other coffee providers, but for now lets hone in on just one of the clever things they've done: the naming of their products.

Before Starbucks came along, your choices were pretty much coffee - regular or large. Some adventurous retailers went out on a limb and also offered extra large. Ooh, exciting.

What did Starbucks do that was different? They gave creative, European sounding names to their drinks, transforming them from a cup of murky 'dullsville' served with a stale donut, to warm, inviting stores where you're served an exciting sounding beverage. You even have the option to create your own exotic concoction.

Consider some of the popular product names at Starbucks...

Frappuccino
Chai Latte
Tazo
Macchiato

Then there are the sizes:

Tall
Grande
Venti

Have you heard about the new mini size at Starbucks? The Tinymissimo. Not really, just kidding. I made it up to make sure you're still paying attention. That would be a nifty name, though.

Then there are the extras:

Java chip
Skinny
Misto
Mocha

Put these words altogether and it's almost a new language, but more importantly it has separated Starbucks from any other coffee chain. Combined with other innovations, they've cleverly made the brand about an *experience* rather than just a cup of coffee – and we should remind ourselves that coffee is a commodity item that's been around since the discovery of caffeine, or is it coffee beans – which came first?!

How to Use This Lesson In Your Business

The lesson to take away is that product names always matter, and they become even more important when you're in a competitive industry.
To show you how this marketing technique can be applied to other industries, lets consider another example.

I recently came across a company that offers wedding videos, the all-important service of capturing the special day.

The company had come up with various options or packages to choose from, each with different benefits and prices. Bizarrley, they named their packages "B" through "H", so there's six options to choose from - "B" being basic (ironically) and "H" being the top of the range, all singing all dancing, everything but the kitchen sink package (my words not theirs).

Besides the fact that six choices is far too many for a wedding video service (a confused mind doesn't buy), and also setting aside the fact that option "A" seems to have mysteriously disappeared from the lineup, think about this company's decision to name their packages with letters of the alphabet. How uninspiring! How lazy! To reduce a service that's inherently creative and important to mere letters of the alphabet is unforgiveable!

Now compare that example with another wedding video company that's obviously given careful thought to the naming process, coming up with creative names to help sell the same service. They offer:

Classic
Prestige
Platinum
Cinematic

These names sound professional, romantic, even exciting. What a difference! If the two businesses were presented side by side, the simple act of using creative names makes the latter stand out from the crowd in a compelling way.

14

Here's how the names are presented in a chart format:

	Classic SD	Prestige SD	Platinum HD	Cinematic HD
Pre-wedding consultation meeting	*	*	*	*
Attend Rehearsal	*	*	*	*
Film Bride preparing on wedding day (optional)	*	*	*	*
Preparations at Ceremony location	*	*	*	*
Pre Ceremony Video Montage	*	*	*	*
Interlude Video Montage		*	*	*
High Quality Digital Editing (at least 80 hours)	*	*	*	*
Filming at Other Locations Included	1	3	3	no limit
Maximum Number of Hours total filming on day	6	8	10	no limit
VHS Copies included	1	1	2	4
Fully Produced DVD included (with custom menu)	1	3	4	10
Number of Cameras used to film ceremony	2	2	2	2
Number of Cameras used to film reception	1	2	1	2
Dolby Digital 5.1 Sound		*	*	*
Standard Definition Cameras Used	*	*	n/a	n/a
High Definition (HD) Cameras Used			*	*
16:9 Filming for Wide Screen TV	on request	on request	*	*
Wedding Day Highlights Compilation		*		*
Photo Montage (no. of pictures)				40
Package Price	**$2745**	**$3495**	**$5495**	**$6995**

Product names should never be an afterthought, a quick two-minute decision before the brochure goes to print, or just because the website designer is breathing down your neck for a decision. Names should be carefully considered, thinking about how you can separate yourself from the competition.

Stand out from the crowd, and customers won't even see the crowd. That's what happened with Starbucks, and that's what can happen to you, in your industry.

Chapter 3

Virgin Airlines

Virgin Airlines is one of serial entrepreneur Sir Richard Branson's companies, and before we get to the big lesson, let's review what Virgin has accomplished as a relative newcomer to the world of aviation.

Virgin Atlantic, the first Virgin airline brand, entered the industry in the UK as "David", versus the long-standing, "Goliath" of British Airways. B.A. appears to have had a track record of using every means possible to crush little 'upstart' airlines in a 'how dare you step on our territory' style of military operation. Many in the region remember Laker Airlines as one such casualty.

So, all the odds were stacked against Virgin succeeding. Yet, fast forward to today and Virgin Atlantic, Virgin America, and Virgin Australia are now the preferred choice by countless passengers around the world. Many people will happily fly on Virgin even when a fare is significantly more expensive than other carriers.

So how did they achieve success despite all the odds?

Fundamentally, Virgin defied the traditional approach that most other airlines have conformed to. And here's the key point:

They asked potential customers what they wanted.

Now there's a novel idea, ask potential customers what they *want*, rather than giving them what YOU think they *need*. How do you know what they want? As an example, Branson himself is well known for hanging out in the economy section of his planes to listen carefully to feedback from passengers. What do they like? What could be better? What are their frustrations? What would make the trip more enjoyable? When was the last time an airline executive consulted you in that manner? I think I can predict the answer.

I happen to be a top-level flyer with a major U.S. airline, not out of choice, but due to the fact that my local airport is dominated by the airline as it's their hub. In other words, I really don't have a choice other than to fly to another hub first, which is impractical and too costly.

Anyway, as I'm in the top 4% of their frequent flyers, and most likely use their service far more than most of their decision making management, you would think that they'd want to hear my suggestions about what works, and what doesn't. How many times do you think I've been invited to provide input in the shaping of future products and services, or even to hear my suggestions on what can be improved now? Sadly, it's never happened.

Years before the Virgin Atlantic brand was born, Richard Branson did his own research informally while travelling on other airlines. They told him and other Virgin researchers that they were easily bored on long flights, so Virgin listened and they were the first to introduce seat-back TV's. This was an obvious innovation in hindsight, yet over thirty years later there are still countless 'modern' airlines that continue to use discolored, fuzzy TV's that

17

drop down from the bulkhead, six rows in front of where passengers sit, squinting to try and see anything!

Airline customers also said it would be cool to have ice cream treats during a long flight, so Virgin introduced ice cream for all passengers.

Customers said they wanted more choices of meals in economy, so Virgin provided three choices when most airlines had two choices or zero choice.

Customers said that they wanted a cabin that was better than economy but not as expensive as business class, so they innovated and implemented premium economy.

Any other airline could have done those things, and subsequently some have begrudgingly followed Virgin's lead, but Virgin were the ones that made the discoveries first, because *they asked, they listened, and they acted fast.*

And the listening has continued. When Virgin America, a newer brand in the Virgin empire, were planning their services in the United States, they didn't rely on past research or knowledge. Again, they took the time to ask prospective customers what they wanted. People said they didn't like the industrial, functional look inside planes, so Virgin designed soft mood lighting, they made the bathrooms more comfortable, and they installed leather seats throughout. People also said that they wanted power for their laptops, so guess what? In went the power outlets throughout the planes, even in economy class.

People also said they were willing to pay for food if it was good quality, but they didn't like the carts coming down the aisles - they blocked the aisle, they bumped into passengers arms and legs, and the food was rarely offered at a time when they wanted it. What did Virgin do? They got rid of the carts - (know anyone that wants to buy a wholesale lot of a food carts)? Then, they designed a menu system on the large, seat-back TVs so passengers can order food and drink whenever they want it, and it's delivered right to their seat. A simple, and brilliant solution!

How to Use This Lesson In Your Business

If Virgin can transform the incredibly competitive airline industry, then you can revolutionize your industry. Sure, the scale is different, but dare to be different, break the rules and deliver something much better to your customers. Throw the typical industry norms out the window and give people what they really want.

How do you know what they want? Ask them.

Use SurveyMonkey.com or a similar tool and create a list of questions. As a result of the feedback Virgin received, they challenged every aspect of the traditional flying experience and created something that's miles ahead of most of the competition. And even though other airlines could have asked their customers to the same extent that Virgin has, they haven't done that. That says it all. They don't want to. They want to continue doing things as they've always done them. Well, they'll continue to get the same results. Just look at the bankruptcies that are going on, airlines continue to drop like flies, while Virgin are smiling all the way to the bank.

Chapter 4

Universal Studios

Universal Studios is best known as a movie distributor, but their other business is a theme park empire. If you haven't been to a Universal Studios, it's kind of like a grown-up version of Disney. It's still a lot of fun, but I think it's more for adults. Don't get me wrong, I love Disney, but at the end of a day of hearing, "it's a small world" a hundred times, and listening to kids who've become screaming brats due to an overdose of sugary treats, I'm just about ready to throttle the first Mickey Mouse I come across.

Anyway, back to Universal...

They do a great job at instant up-sells at the ticket booth, and that's what this big lesson is about.

First of all, at certain times of the year, an annual pass is only $10 more than a one-day admission. Now, that's an irresistible offer. If you're wondering how they can afford to do that, remember that Universal extracts a lot of money from every visitor beyond the admission price. Once you're inside the park, there's the food & drink, the souvenirs, the ponchos to protect you on the water rides, and so on.

The next up-sell opportunity is for what Universal calls, "the front of the line pass." What a great idea. You get priority access to all rides and attractions, reserved seating at the shows, and a few other nifty benefits. And let's face it, who wouldn't want to bypass the long lines that are notorious at theme parks?

Then there's an up-sell that appeals to the stomach. It's the "all you can eat" pass, for $19.95. There are some conditions to dissuade the selfish minority from abusing the system with gluttony, but it's still a great deal if you plan to stay in the park all day.

So, Universal offers three different up-sells, at least at the time of writing that was the case.

How to Use This Lesson In Your Business

From this example, there are four (count 'em) lessons you can apply to your business. I know, you were only expecting one, but I do like to over deliver and surprise you, so four it is.

First, *have at least one up-sell.* That's easy to fix, and you'll increase your profits overnight. Many businesses offer a range of products or services, with a take it or leave it attitude. Did you know that the hottest time to sell to a customer is immediately after they've committed to a first purchase? It's true. That's why upsells can be so effective.

Second, make the up-sell *relevant to the main product.* Imagine if you went to McDonald's, ordered a Big Mac and they said, "would you like a stapler with that?" It's not relevant, and they wouldn't get many sales, obviously. So, there needs to be a logical tie-in with the main product.

Third, create an *irresistible offer.* An annual pass for $10 more than a one-day ticket is an irresistible offer, it represents incredible value, and lots of people upgrade as a result. So give careful thought to your offers and make them as compelling as possible. You shouldn't have to do a lot of explaining, cajoling, influencing, or persuading; if it's irresistible it will virtually sell itself.

Last, *an up-sell shouldn't be a hard sell.* Make the offer clear and let the customer decide, don't hassle them. Like me, you've probably experienced a high-pressure sales person who tried to get you to spend money on upgrades that you simply weren't interested in. For example, car dealers are notorious for up-selling customers into high-priced protection treatments or replacement key services at a far higher cost than they would normally be if you bought those services independently afterwards. That's an example of how NOT to do an up-sell.

If possible, offer a money-back guarantee to reassure customers that they're making a good decision. Interestingly, at Universal, most customers approach the window and *ask* for the add-on offers directly, because they're presented in a clear, non-confrontational way. As business author Jeffrey Gitomer likes to say, "people love to buy, but they don't like to be sold to".

Also, keep in mind that at Universal Studios, the customers are already waiting in line when they see the offers - in other words, they're already committed to buying a ticket, and Universal simply slots in some extra options for them to consider. The positioning of the offers is, "you've made a good decision already. Now have you thought about adding these options?" That's a great way to handle up-sells.

Review the four key points in this chapter and examine whether you're implementing them effectively in your own business.

22

Chapter 5

Norwegian Cruise Line

Norwegian Cruise Line, also known as NCL, is a popular cruise company positioned and priced in the mid-range of offerings. They're not the cheapest, nor the most expensive, but somewhere in between.

Although the cruise industry is a competitive niche, NCL's business is booming, because they're marketing to and attracting a completely different type of customer from the 'norm', combined with strategically having the youngest fleet of ships in the entire industry.

What did they do? They looked at trends and realized that there was a new demographic of cruisers that was increasing in size consistently and rapidly - young couples and families - who liked the idea of cruising, but they didn't like the traditional cruise experience.

My wife Luci and I, consider ourselves in this same demographic. When we cruise, we don't want to eat at a set time, in one restaurant. I don't want to be told to dress up in a tuxedo. We don't like the forced tipping policy, and frankly, everything is far too formal on most cruise lines. Not that we wanted a rowdy experience, we didn't. We just wanted a relaxed environment with a lot more choices and a lot less dictated to us, as in, "you will be down for dinner at 4:00 p.m." We don't even have lunch until 4:00 p.m. on some days! As you can see, we know what we want (call me a Diva if you like, I don't mind) and the traditional cruise lines weren't providing that.

The big cheeses at NCL are very smart. They went against the traditional, stuffy cruise line image, and created what they call 'FreeStyle Cruising'. As a result, they've made themselves unique in the industry, and for many people, there's no other choice for a cruise. Luci and I have cruised eleven times with them now.

As an example of the freestyle concept, the ship we most recently sailed on had thirteen different restaurants! There was a steak house, French, Italian, Asian, Teppanyaki, Tapas, Fast Food burger bar, and so on. On any given day we could turn up at a restaurant anytime from 5pm until 10pm.

We never had to sit on a table with eight complete strangers (unless we wanted to), and the servers didn't fish for tips. It's our kind of cruise, and there are plenty of other people who feel the same way, who now cruise with NCL.

How to Use This Lesson In Your Business

The lesson here for your business is to challenge industry norms. There's always more than one way of doing things, and a good starting point is to *think about doing the opposite of what others are doing.*

When NCL announced freestyle cruising, the other cruise lines were quick to mock NCL. They said it'll never work, they said that the traditional approach had worked for over a hundred years, and so on. Very narrow minded, and its what you'd expect from an industry that's bogged down with stuffiness, and seen little innovation.

By challenging convention, often you can open up your business to a new set of customers, and further separate yourself from the competition. Right now, most cruise lines are very similar. NCL really stands out from the crowd, and that's a very good thing.

Chapter 6

McDonald's

Here's a company that needs no introduction. We all know about the burgers and fries, but did you know that McDonald's truly is the giant of the fast food industry, with more than 30,000 restaurants in more than 100 countries? That's right, millions of people have been super-sized! So why has McDonald's been so successful, despite the fact that many other fast-food chains clearly have better quality food? In case you're interested, my personal favorites are Wendy's and In-N-Out.

The key to McDonald's success is in one word: systems. They have a system for every aspect of their business, and it's a finely tuned approach that's repeated in every store from Austria to Adelaide.

Most people don't realize that McDonald's entire business revolves around systems. From the very start, founder Ray Kroc was obsessed with developing systems; he even named the company *McDonald's Systems Incorporated.* Ray was smart in realizing that if he was going to expand the business, nothing could be left to chance. Everything needed to be replicated over and over again in an exact manner, in any part of the country, and eventually any part of the world.

Ray thought of everything. Things like finding out the maximum number of hamburgers they could stack in a box without squishing them, or the number of seconds that could be saved if they used buns that were pre-sliced all the way through, rather than being stuck together. They even considered the best place to position the drinks machines, cups, and lids, so all staff can reach them easily within a couple of steps of wherever they're serving, for maximum efficiency and minimum time and frustration. Those things all became part of a grand system. Every McDonald's in the world now uses that same system.

McDonald's also created *Hamburger University* to ensure that every staff member receives consistent training. Nothing is left to chance, including the words that staff members use to politely ask for an order. The same words are used in every restaurant – test this yourself and you'll see this to be true.

This obsession with systems means that even an inexperienced newcomer in their 20's can *manage* a McDonald's restaurant, and most of us have witnessed that first hand, a puzzling sight to be sure. You ask to speak to the manager and someone who look like your son comes over and asks how they can help. Very disconcerting. Still, it works. They get the training, they get the manuals with all the systems, they follow them step-by-step, and it works.

How to Use This Lesson In Your Business

Sadly, most small business owners don't have a system for anything. So the first lesson is to **recognize that you need systems.**

Here's what to do first: grab a notepad and jot down the processes that you do regularly, say once a day, week, or month, and write those down. Next, make a note of any single process you've done in the past that has brought good results. Those things should also be tweaked for maximum effectiveness and included in a grand system. Logically, if it worked before, it should be repeated over and over again.

Also, make a note of the end results you want. Once you know where you're heading, you can work back to figure out what you need to do to get those results. Those elements will eventually become your system.

Personally, having systems has been one of the big breakthroughs in my business, and that's why I'm such a big fan of them.

You may or may not be aware that I have a marketing vault that I have opened up to entrepreneurs to benefit from. It's full of pre-made marketing systems you can copy to improve your business. Take a look at **www.HelpMyBusiness.com** for more details, and a special offer.

Chapter 7

IKEA

This big marketing lesson is from IKEA, the Swedish-based furniture company. IKEA has mastered the art of turning negatives into positives.

I'll explain.

IKEA has a lot of negative aspects about their business, i.e. you have to go around a warehouse and collect all the flat packs you need, transport those large boxes home yourself, and assemble the furniture in your own time. There are other negatives, but these are at the core of their business.

Let's consider how IKEA handles these issues, cleverly turning negatives into positives.

First, they established a brand that conveys the message: "we offer quality at low prices". They say, "You do your part, we do ours, and together we save money." They present this message consistently in the catalog, in stores, on signage, and so on. Every customer is well educated as to *why* they're getting a good deal.

Here's an excerpt from an IKEA catalog:

"Shopping is a bit different at the IKEA store. We ask you to share in some of the work. At the store you pick up what you want and take everything home and put it together yourself.

Why do we do this? To offer you low prices.

Doing the work yourself means you don't have to pay someone else to do it for you. It's a little extra effort from you that makes a big difference to the price.

And we have to do some extra work for low prices, too. We pack things flat to save on transport and storage, we choose manufacturers who can deliver quality at a low price, we buy in big quantities."

Can you see how clever that positioning is? What would normally cause people to be irritated is repositioned as a positive.

How to Use This Lesson In Your Business

What perceived negatives can you turn around in your business?

It's surprisingly simple to re-frame negatives to make them appealing as benefits, rather than weaknesses. For example, my dad supplies and fits kitchens, but he's a one-man operation competing against large, national companies with big buying power. My dad turned a perceived negative into a positive by telling customers that throughout the entire process from the initial consultation to the fitting, they get to deal with just one person. And guess what, many people immediately change their perception to see him (the little guy) as the better deal because they'd rather pay more and get personalized service rather than being passed through six or seven people and treated as just "customer number 4352".

The lesson to take away is that you can always turn negatives into positives, to make your business stand out from the crowd.

Chapter 8

amazon.com.

Amazon.com

This big marketing lesson is from Amazon.com. Amazon does a lot of things right, but the single lesson I want to focus on for this chapter is their Amazon Prime program. They've really nailed it.

For under $100 a year, when you buy any item that Amazon ships directly (which is most items on the site) you get unlimited two day shipping for free, or overnight shipping anywhere in the U.S. for just $3.99. And one membership is good for the whole household.

The service is obviously aimed at people who buy regularly online, and those people quickly develop the habit of shopping at Amazon.com in preference to any other online retailer. It's a fantastically simple loyalty program that keeps customers coming back over and over again throughout the year.

In addition, Amazon Prime includes the ability to watch some movies on demand, using their streaming video service. This is an added value, and also gets more people familiar with their service, increasing the likelihood of them buying other TV or movie titles from the catalog.

Contrasting Amazon Prime with an example of what *not* to do, I signed up for a loyalty program with another site called, eCost.com, which is now as dead as a dodo. They promised free ground shipping, discounted express shipping, and access to exclusive special offers. That all sounds great, right? I paid the fee, placed an order, and sadly, that's where the problems started.

Instead of being treated like a valued customer, I was charged full shipping cost on my first two membership orders, the "exclusive offers" were disappointing and could hardly qualify as 'special', and when I tried to contact the company, my emails were all left unanswered. Needless to say, I never went back to eCost, and they're now out of business.

How to Use This Lesson In Your Business

If you don't have a loyalty program, you may want to consider it. But don't mess it up. Keep it simple, make sure it works exactly as promised. Don't try and profit directly from any fees you charge for the program. It's okay to charge a fee as long as the value can to the customer is obvious, and it represents far more than any amount they pay you to be a member.

The bottom line is, use a loyalty program *as a tool to encourage customers to place more orders*. Do it right, and they'll do just that.

My Amazon orders have at least quadrupled in number since I joined Prime, and friends all say the same. I love it. They love it. We all love it. There's a lot of Amazon lovin' going on.

Chapter 9
CIRQUE DU SOLEIL.

Cirque Du Soleil

Cirque Du Soleil has almost twenty shows going on at the same time all over the world, including eight permanent shows in Las Vegas: Mystere, Ka, Zumanity, O, Love, Criss Angel's Believe, Michael Jackson's ONE, and Zarkana.

Now, how do you describe what Cirque du Soleil is to someone who hasn't seen one of their shows? It's really difficult. I'll take a stab at it: it's a live performance that appeals to a wide audience; there's live music, comedy, theatrics and spectacle, and no dialogue. The shows are an assault on your senses, and they feature the best circus style performers in the world. Oh, and they don't use any live animals. The company originated in Canada, and there's definitely a quirky French twist or flavor to many of the productions.

The major lesson we can take away from Cirque du Soleil is how they adapted the declining circus industry to create something new, and much more appealing, that has subsequently taken the world by storm.

Cirque removed the aspects that people didn't like about the circus and replaced them with new innovations that enhanced the experience. So, out went the animals (sorry Leo the lion and Tony the tiger), out went the distracting vendors in the aisles selling ridiculously overpriced peanuts and popcorn, out went the three rings of the traditional circus, and out went well known 'star' performers.

The creators of Cirque felt that all of those elements were unnecessary and even past their prime. Instead, they created a much more refined experience, with a central theme, live music, stunning production elements, creative costumes, ground breaking staging and lighting, all in a tent or a uniquely designed building.

To define it further, Cirque created something of a cross between circus and theater, and that new positioning also meant that they could charge prices that were four or five times higher than the circus!

This really is a genius strategy, and the results speak for themselves. Circuses continue to decline in popularity while Cirque du Soleil continues to grow at a phenomenal rate.

How to Use This Lesson In Your Business

Be bold in challenging the way things have been done for years in your industry. Circuses have been around for countless years, yet someone still came along and reinvented them with a few well thought out tweaks. They looked at every aspect of the traditional model and noted what customers disliked about it. It's amazing how that simple process can lead to incredible innovation, even the formation of a new niche.

Be bold in challenging things you don't like about your existing business, and look for a better way, which can often be found by looking outside your industry. Oh, and by the way, if you haven't seen a Cirque show, I highly recommend it.

Chapter 10

Wal-Mart

This BIG marketing lesson is from Wal-Mart. The challenge with Wal-Mart's business is that most of their items are commodity products that customers can buy from any other store. And competing primarily on price is never a good idea because history has proven that everyone loses in the long run.

Wal-Mart, to their credit, have employed a smart marketing concept called bundling – it's where you put another product with the main product to make it different (and better) than what other stores are selling. A good example is this DVD pack:

Rather than selling the DVD on its own as all the other stores do, Wal-Mart had the studio create a bonus DVD with behind the scenes footage, exclusive to Wal-Mart. They then bundled the extra DVD with the regular DVD to create a new product, one that no one else could offer. Total extra cost was probably around 50 cents a piece. And when buyers compare the exclusive Wal-Mart bundle with the regular DVD from any other store, which one do you think they go for? The answer is obvious - the Wal-Mart bundle drives many more sales.

How to Use This Lesson In Your Business

In your business, what can you add to an existing product to create a bundle?

Remember, a bundle is instantly more attractive to most buyers because they're getting better value, and it's also a perfect way to stand out from the crowd, especially with commodity products that shoppers know they can buy from a range of similar stores.

To use another example, suppose that you're selling toothbrushes, a competitive item that you can get from countless stores. However, each toothbrush could be bundled with a sample of a toothpaste, or some toothpicks, or perhaps a flossing tool. Get the idea? By adding other items into the mix, you instantly create more value, and avoid an apples to apples comparison.

Chapter 11

Costco

This big marketing lesson is from Costco, the warehouse company that sells just about everything you can think of, at a great price, as long as you buy at least forty of them.

In all seriousness, I love Costco. Their management has a really deep understanding of what people want, and the company has a great reputation.

Let's look at their refund policy...

Most companies have a vague, weasely, or limiting return policy. Not so with Costco. Oh no. Costco allows you to return almost anything up to three months after the purchase, for a full refund. You don't even need the receipt. Also, on electronics goods they automatically extend warranties from one year to two years, and they offer a dedicated technical support line for free.

Now that's a return policy.

Do some people abuse it? Of course they do. It's funny how many 70" TVs are returned just after the Super bowl weekend. But even though the policy is abused, many more people recommend Costco to their friends because of how generous it is. Ultimately, it gives buyers confidence to shop there.

How to Use This Lesson In Your Business

What's your return policy if you sell physical products? Think about this...if you're in a competitive business you could make your return policy a *unique selling proposition*, as a way to make you stand out from the crowd.

Ideally, get the manufacturer to take the risk, not you, but either way don't be afraid of promising more than your competitors do. Make a big deal about your refund policy, and you'll see many more customers choosing to do business with you.

Unfortunately, fair return policies are few and far between these days. Be bold, and offer something better - a Costco style return policy. It's sure to bring you more business.

Chapter 12

the web's most popular shoe store!®

Zappos.Com

This big marketing lesson is from Zappos.com. On the surface, Zappos seems like an odd business - a business that probably never would have been started if it had been in the hands of a traditional Board of Directors. Zappos sells shoes - online. Just think about that. It doesn't seem the best business to be operating online, does it?

Well, Zappos has achieved phenomenal success by doing just that. The company overcame all the obvious objections and created a business that now does over a billion dollars in sales each year.

It's a fascinating example to consider, because all the odds were against them succeeding.

I met Tony Hsieh, the CEO of Zappos, and he commented that one of the things that made Zappos grow really fast is their shipping policy. They really went out on a limb to offer *free shipping both ways*. They encourage their customers to order as many shoes as they want, try them at home, and send back the ones they don't like, for free.

This is a brilliant strategy because it removes one of the most consistent barriers to online sales – the shipping costs. No one likes paying shipping for anything online.

With their business model of buying inventory directly from manufacturers (saving lots of money in the process), Zappos realized that it would be viable to offer free shipping.

How to Use This Lesson In Your Business

When was the last time you examined your shipping prices, especially if you sell via mail-order, or online? Could your existing shipping policy be a barrier that's preventing more sales? Could your shipping prices be reduced, perhaps going to a fixed price or even a free model like Zappos?

Do you recognize that buyers hate paying shipping? Studies have shown that many people would rather pay more for the item and have it 'include' shipping than have to pay shipping separately.

If you are able to offer free shipping, make a big deal about it. Shout it from the rooftops...not literally - that might get you in trouble, but do use it to your advantage. Free shipping is a big deal, and it's a promise that stands out from the crowd, because most companies are afraid to go down that road.

Zappos reminds customers on every page of their website that they offer free shipping, and it's even written in bright orange text deliberately to stand out. It's one of their key unique selling points, and their phenomenal sales volume and success proves it's working.

Chapter 13

Tiffany & Company

This big marketing lesson is from Tiffany & Company, the jewelry supplier. Can you guess what the lesson is? It's about their product packaging.

Tiffany's famous egg blue box has become synonymous with quality, conveying both luxury and exclusivity.

Interestingly, these boxes tend to be viewed as valuable in their own right, so much so that the receiver of a gift in a Tiffany's box is happy before they even open it! That's an impressive achievement when you think about it. The box has become such an important part of the brand that staff in department stores report that people regularly ask just for a box!

It's also important to note that Tiffany's distinctive packaging has created such a recognizable and trusted brand that the products inside can be sold at higher prices than other stores – and they are. So the Tiffany products aren't necessarily superior, it's the packaging that increases both price and perceived value.

This observation was stated in a more eloquent way by Denise Myer in her independent study of Tiffany's, where she said,

"Tiffany's wants you to forget the product and remember where it came from!"

How true that is. Incidentally, this is yet another example of how everything is marketing and marketing is everything, as I like to say.

Your packaging is a reflection of how you view customers, and they'll be influenced, either positively or negatively about you and your business as a result. The customer experience is subconsciously translated into in a decision about whether to buy from you again. So even packaging is marketing, it matters!

How to Use This Lesson In Your Business

Understand that packaging makes a difference to the customer experience. Over the next few weeks, analyze everything that's sent to you from other businesses, and notice what's good and bad. In other words, look for ideas that you can borrow from other suppliers.

Yes, you can shove a product in a padded mailer jiffy bag and it'll get delivered, but will that wow the customer, or will it simply blend in with the other four packages they received that week?

For a while now, I've been sending products in metallic silver envelopes:

They really stand out from the crowd, and lots of customers make positive comments about them, saying things like "It caught my attention and I was really excited to open it"

A little bit of creative thinking can enable you to present a great first impression to your customers by sending your products in creative packaging. Help customers remember you, and leave them with a positive experience. Do that, and there's a good chance they'll be back for more.

Chapter 14

❂ Blendtec®

Blendtec

This big marketing lesson is from the friendly folks at Blendtec - they sell kitchen blenders from $400 to over $2,000. Kitchen blenders? Yes.

Why are they so expensive? Because they're really, really, good, and they know it. Arguably, Blendtec make the best blenders on the planet, although the people at Vitamix might disagree. Still, if you visit any high-end coffee shop, juice bar, gym or restaurant they're most likely using Blendtec blenders.

The last time I was at Disney World I bought a fruit smoothie, and I was intrigued to see that they were using a huge Blendtec machine that looked like a bit like a replicator device out of Star Trek. The operator pressed a button, and a few seconds later a perfect smoothie was produced, using just the right amount of fruit mixed with just the right amount of ice. Very impressive. These blenders are the best of the best.

So how do you promote something that's really really good, and really really expensive?

Well, one day the company's marketing director was walking through their warehouse and saw the CEO testing a new blender by inserting a large plank of 2"x4" wood into it! That sparked an

45

idea to create videos where they would try to blend all kinds of unusual objects to show how powerful their blenders really are.

The idea quickly became reality and in the last few years they've blended golf balls, highlighter pens, an iPod, an iPhone, a video camera, and even fifty marbles! As you can imagine, it's compulsive viewing, and as a result, many of the videos have gone viral, with millions of people viewing them on YouTube alone. That in turn has resulted in massive sales for Blendtec blenders, to such an extent that the company often has a hard time keeping up with the demand.

How to Use This Lesson In Your Business

Showcase your product in an interesting or entertaining way. It just calls for a little imagination and creativity.

Most marketing is boring, and it repels people. The *'Will it Blend'* videos from Blendtec gave character and personality to what was previously a large, boring, and faceless corporation. Not only that, but they provide powerful proof that the product IS superior to many other blenders.

You should know that the 'Will it blend' videos were produced with a simple camcorder, nothing more. No fancy editing, just a simple, entertaining message.

Maybe you could do a video series called 'will it burn', 'will it melt', 'will it decay', 'will it crush' - you get the idea. The important lesson is to present your product in an unusual, interesting, and entertaining way.

Obviously it depends what your product is – it may or may not be possible to directly use or adapt this concept, but at least think about the principle here.

46

By the way, Blendtec's videos have been so successful that they've created a website to showcase them. Take a look at www.WillitBlend.com, and you can even purchase a DVD of the most popular episodes, complete with outtakes!

Chapter 15

Google™

Google

Google provides this big marketing lesson. In case you're not an Internet user or you've been living in a cave in Siberia for the last 18 years, Google is the #1 search engine online. Come to think of it, if you had been living in a cave in Siberia, you wouldn't even know what a search engine is, would you? Or computers. Or the Internet. Oh well, let's assume you do know what Google is, and we'll go from there.

What made Google grow so popular, so fast? Well, the web was traditionally dominated by large, bloated home pages like MSN, AOL, and Yahoo. Their sites were full of information, lots of choices, and it seemed like it was a competition of who could cram the most stuff on the home page.

The Google guys approached the industry from a completely different perspective. They believed that although they had great search technology, they needed to provide a much simpler interface than was currently being offered. They felt that Internet users were crying out for something more user-friendly. And that's the fundamental key to the success of Google.

Google came along and it was like a breath of fresh air. Normal people like you and me, well at least you, could suddenly search online, easily.

The Google guys had acknowledged that most Internet users are not geeks or nerds, they're regular people who use the Internet as a tool, not as part of a life support system or umbilical cord.

How to Use This Lesson In Your Business

The lesson for your business is this: *keep it simple, and focus on being user friendly.* Most companies tend to over complicate their products, which has a negative impact.

Have you ever heard someone say:

"If only this product was more complicated to use - I wish they would add more buttons, dials, switches, and options!"

Offering something that's simple and user friendly is always a good thing.

Could it be that you have too many inwardly focused techy people in your business, and not enough outwardly reaching advocates? Focus on giving customers something that's genuinely easy to use. Work to the lowest common denominator, rather than pandering to the few people who shout the loudest, or the ones who are like you.

Know your customers, and serve them with a product that's simple to understand and simple to use. I've never seen any business over simplify a product or service – generally the opposite tends to be true.

Chapter 16

UPS

This big marketing lesson is from UPS. Now, this is an unusual one because it focuses on learning from what UPS does *poorly*, rather than a positive example.

I sent about twenty boxes of DVD's to someone using a UPS store, and it was an important shipment so I fully insured it against every possibility. Well, as it happened, UPS lost the entire shipment.

Now, here's the really bad part. When I went to submit the claim, I found out that it had to be done through the local store where I'd shipped the packages from.

It turned out, the staff at the store had no knowledge of how to process a claim, and the owner of the store was difficult to reach to ask for guidance. When I finally managed to contact him, he refused to honor the claim, giving all kinds of excuses.

My only recourse at that point was to ask for help from the UPS UPS main corporate office. So I called them up and astonishingly the representative I spoke with told me:

50

"We have no control over UPS stores, they're independent franchises."

I pointed out that there's a large brown sign over the top of each store that says 'UPS', which means they *are* controlled in some manner by UPS.

After much unsuccessful and frustrating wrangling, the bottom line was, all UPS were willing to do was to add a note on the franchise owners account to say that I was unhappy with their service!

Can you believe that?

How to Use This Lesson In Your Business

In a nutshell, this is about *retaining control.* If you have to outsource some aspect of your business, you must retain some level of control to ensure that customers who interact with your brand are treated well.

My experience proves what can happen when companies just look at the dollar signs and fail to maintain their business at a certain standard.

Nowadays I only use FedEx, and I'm delighted with the service they provide. Ironically, it's not even any more expensive because I negotiated favorable rates. I will never go back to UPS, that's how bad my experience was with them. They lost a good customer, I've also now told you about what happened, and you'll probably tell others, too.

It's vital to keep a careful eye on other people who serve your customers, because if they don't care as much as you do, they can do enormous damage to your business and reputation.

51

Incidentally, as an aside, I've also discovered that the U.S. Postal Service (USPS) international insurance is not worth the paper it's written on. Many postal workers I've spoken with have acknowledged that through their own experience and observations, and I learned it the hard way, too.

I had an insurance claim with USPS that went on for more than a year. I jumped through all their hoops, produced all the evidence they asked for, and when it came down to it they still refused to honor the claim. So now we never send important packages via USPS now, either. It's Fedex or nothing. Fedex wins by default.

Chapter 17

Excedrin

Excedrin

This big marketing lesson is from Excedrin, the popular brand of headache tablets. Let's play a little game here - spot the difference:

 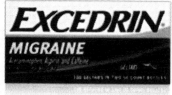

One pack is green, one is red. Very good, that's a start. Now look at the label - one is 'extra strength,' the other is 'migraine' formula. One is caplets (whatever that means), the other is tablets.

Now, here's the really interesting part. Look at the ingredients. Both products list Acetaminophen - 250mg, they both have Aspirin - 250mg, and they both have Caffeine - 65mg. That's right, the ingredients are identical, so they're identical products.

Why have they done this? Well, did you know that there are in fact, lots of types of headaches? It's true! There are tension headaches; migraine headaches; cluster headaches; sinus headaches; there are even headaches from diving into a swimming pool when it's been emptied for maintenance! That's called a permanent headache!

Here's the deal...

When a company offers *a solution that appears to closely match the problem*, customers are much more inclined to buy that product, in preference to other more 'general' products.

As another example, if you're experiencing an infestation of ants in your home, you'll most likely head down to the local store to buy a product to fix that problem. As you scan the shelves, you see a variety of insect killing products, as well as dedicated ant killing powder. Which do you buy? The stats prove that ant killer wins consistently. Why? Because *it's perceived to be a more specific solution*, even though the ingredients in the insect killer product may have been identical. Interesting psychology, isn't it?

How to Use This Lesson In Your Business

Recognize that *the closer you can match your product or service to specific needs or audiences, the better your sales will be*. As we've proved here, you don't even need to change the ingredients of a product, you simply change the positioning and the promotion.

To give you another example, I sell a course in using eBay for lead generation. Any business can use that course, but if I speak to a group of Doctors, I rebrand the course as 'The H3 eBay System for Doctors'. I might put a picture of a stethoscope, or a bedpan, or someone fainting on the cover, but it's the same product, rebranded for a specific audience of buyers. It really works! Oh, and also note that when I rebrand a course, it always sells for a higher price than if I were to offer the generic version.

Look out for opportunities to re-position your product for other audiences.

If you sell printing services and you find that most of your work is for lawyers, you could reposition your business as *the* printer for lawyers. You'll probably attract most of the other lawyers in town, because people prefer to deal with specialists who they believe understand their needs.

Truthfully, you very well might have experience in dealing with lawyers that *does* make you better able to help them compared with other printers, which is all the more reason to specialize.

Of course, this is just an example. Don't get stuck on the details, understand the principle here.

Rebranding, repositioning, whatever you want to call it, is an easy way to attract more business, because when the customer feels that your solution is *perfect for them*, they're much more inclined to buy from you.

Chapter 18

Hard Rock Café

I was visiting Universal Studios in Hollywood, and I went for lunch at the Hard Rock Cafe in the plaza area.

It's been a few years since I've been to a Hard Rock restaurant and I was very impressed. Not only was the food much better quality than the average entertainment themed restaurant, the service was great too; it was exceptional service, actually.

More than that, it was a memorable experience. First, you have all the interesting music memorabilia around the walls - that makes for interesting conversation while you're waiting. Then there's the store inside the restaurant. That makes it easy for guests to browse and buy.

I ordered a drink in a souvenir glass, and at the end of the meal the server bought a clean glass, wrapped up nicely, so that I didn't have to take the dirty glass with me - a nice touch.

The lesson here is to *create a theme and an experience for your customers.*

The Hard Rock cafe is just a restaurant, but they've managed to transform their business into an experience by creating a theme.

Could you create a theme for your business - something that'll get people talking about it?

It might seem like the Hard Rock Café was in a unique position to create a theme? Well, remember, it's a restaurant, which is a very crowded industry. The theme makes it special, and captures peoples attention.

Is it really possible to do the same thing for other 'boring' businesses?

How about Dentists? There's not much to separate one from another, is there?

Well, I came across a dental practice that's themed around Star Trek - it's called **Starbase Dental** in Orlando, and as you can imagine, a lot of kids love to go there. Actually, a lot of adults love to go there, too!

Each chair is styled like one of the chairs from the bridge of the enterprise, and the patients can watch episodes of Star Trek on a TV monitor placed above their head.

Think about what Starbase Dental has accomplished. Do customers keep coming back? Yes! Is the higher price they charge a big deal to their customers? Not at all. Do people talk about it to their friends? Yes!

Starbase Dental has no problem whatsoever getting new clients, even in a recession. *They've created a unique, memorable experience.*

How to Use This Lesson In Your Business

Challenge what's considered normal in your industry and don't be afraid to create a theme, and by extension an experience.

If you have created an interesting theme for your business, or you know of someone else who's done that, I'd love to know about it. Please send an email with a description of the business and theme, to andrew@helpmybusiness.com, and I may feature it in a future episode of my WebTV show, "Help My Business!" (visit **www.HelpMyBusiness.com** to view the show.)

Chapter 19

In-n-Out

In-N-Out is a popular fast food chain in certain states in the USA. If you live in California, Arizona, or Utah, you'll already know that In-N-Out has a large, loyal following. The restaurants are known for fresh, tasty food, made to order, along with a simple menu in a clean environment. It's a formula that's served them well for many years, but there's another ingredient that's quite unique...

It's the secret menu.

What's the secret menu? Well, it wouldn't be a secret if I told you, now would it? Just teasing. I'll happily spill the beans for you, my fellow entrepreneur...

There's a number of items that you won't find advertised anywhere on an In-N-Out menu board, yet many customers know about them. That's a pretty nifty idea. Why? Because it encourages a kind of word of mouth viral marketing, as in: "Hey, did you know about the secret menu at In-N-Out? Yeah, you can order a double, double protein style."

How to Use This Lesson In Your Business

How can you use this concept in your business? Well, knowing that people want to be in on a secret, *what secret could you 'accidentally leak' about your business that would get people talking?*

Ideally, you want to make it a secret that makes the person feel special, like an insider. For example, how about a code word where customers get 10% off for using it?

Imagine a friend telling you:

"Hey, did you know that if you go into a Starbucks and say the word 'wigwam' when you order, they'll give you 10% off?"

"No way!" you say.

"Yes, way" they say.

I'd try it, wouldn't you? And when it worked, you'd tell everyone! There'd be people saying "wigwam" all over town!

By the way, that's just an example - please *don't* go into Starbucks and say "wigwam" because all you'll get is a funny look. But do take this principle and apply it to your business.

Create a special secret that will easily get spread among your customers. It's a great way to encourage them to talk about your business in a positive way.

Chapter 20

Häagen Dazs

Häagen Dazs is of course a well-known purveyor of fine ice-cream. The name is very distinctive, isn't it? Any idea where the company was founded? Denmark perhaps? Sweden? Finland? Sorry to break it to you, but the answer is The Bronx, New York. Yes, Häagen Dazs is about as Scandinavian as the New York Jets.

The words Häagen Dazs literally translated mean 'pretentiously priced ice-cream' - just kidding, actually the words 'Häagen Dazs' aren't even pronounceable in any Scandinavian language! Like I said, the company was established in the Bronx, and is now based New Jersey. Sorry to disappoint. Impressive though, isn't it?

Actually Häagen Dazs is by no means the only company to use creative naming to imply a connection that isn't actually there. In the UK for example, the large electronics chain Dixons promotes an in-house brand of electronics called *'Matsui'* – it sounds Japanese but it's not. Then there's *Dolmio Sauce* sold by Masterfoods. It sounds Italian, but you won't find it sold in any Italian stores. Again, the name was strategically invented.

61

How to Use This Lesson In Your Business

The lesson here is that *it's sometimes useful to associate a product with an established stereotype.*

I'm sure you can relate to the fact that Germany is associated with expensive high-end cars, Japan with electronics, Italy with shoes, fashion and style, France with cosmetics, perfumes, and gourmet food, Russia with vodka and caviar, Switzerland with precision watches, and so on. Actually, I was just thinking about what England is associated with - football hooligans perhaps? Wonderful! London smog maybe? A cup of tea? Warm beer? Rain? Stuffy traditions?

Anyway, I digress.

Let's get practical.

Could you rename some of your products to tie in with some useful, established perceptions?

If you run a pizza restaurant, instead of boring, uninspiring names like 'ham and pineapple' could you offer the *'Prosciutto Perfection'* pizza?

Instead of the 'watch repair store', how about *'The Swiss Timepiece Service Center'.*

Get the idea? Get creative, you'll stand out from the crowd, and you'll also be able to charge premium prices.

Chapter 21

Vistaprint

Vistaprint, an online printing company, have dominated the world of printing for small business through a simple and very clever viral marketing strategy. They offer free business cards with one small catch - the back of the card has the message:

"Business Cards are free at Vistaprint.com!"

They've printed more than three billion cards with that message, which means that hundreds of thousands of people, possibly even millions, have responded and ordered products from Vistaprint for their own businesses, while promoting the Vistaprint brand at the same time. What's even more impressive, is that this strategy appears to cost Vistaprint nothing! Why? Because their shipping and handling charge on the 'free' cards more than covers their costs!

Incidentally, as a side note, and I need to get this off my chest because it really irritates me, if you're in business and you can't afford $10 or whatever paltry sum it is to have the 'printed by Vistaprint' text removed, what kind of message does that send out to your prospective customers?! They're more likely to take notice of the creative way that Vistaprint marketed themselves on the back of your card, and ignore your marketing message, because you apparently don't believe in your business enough to spend $10 on it. Okay, end of rant!

How to Use This Lesson In Your Business

Learning from the principle here, *what could you create that costs you little or nothing, and that gets your marketing message seen by a lot more people?*

One industry that does this already is car dealers. When you buy a car, what do they put in the back window or on the license plate or bumper? We've all seen it. They put some kind of decal that promotes themselves, such as: "Another fine vehicle from Austin Audi" - that kind of thing.

Here's another example. I was given this card on a British Airways flight:

It's a fun puzzle, but it also promotes Westin, the hotel chain.

Think creatively about your industry and see what you can come up with as an inexpensive or free tool to get your business seen by many more people.

64

Chapter 22

easyCar.com

EasyCar

EasyCar is a popular British car rental company. EasyCar is unique in a number of ways. First, they ask their customers to return the car clean. In fact, it's a requirement that's clearly written on the side of the vehicle. Even the rental agreement says something along the lines of, "…if you choose not to bring your car back clean, EasyCar will perform this task on your behalf and apply a £10 charge" (that's about $18).

According to the company, about 85% of their customers bring the car back clean, and presumably the rest are happy to pay the extra charge to have someone else do it for them.

That simple, "bring the car back clean" policy has saved substantial costs for EasyCar. Not only do they need a lot less staff to clean cars, but the cars can also be rented much more quickly to new customers, because they don't have to be sent through a time-consuming cleaning process.

How to Use This Lesson In Your Business

The lesson for your business is to **outsource certain costs to your customers, and position it as an advantage!** That might sound crazy, but you've just read about how EasyCar did just that!

It requires some out of the box thinking to break industry norms, but why not?

Here's another example to consider.

Seminar speakers usually include transportation and hotel costs when quoting for a gig. However, if they remove that and simply state, 'travel and accommodation costs to be covered by client', they save themselves time in researching those costs, and their quotation is also lower. Since many corporations have in-house travel departments, they'll usually be happy to arrange that aspect of the gig.

Again, the lesson is to *remove costs that can be outsourced to the client, and then position that as a benefit.* It's an advanced strategy, but do it right and it's a win-win for both you and your customers.

Chapter 23

Threadless.Com

Threadless.com is a company that makes T-shirts - some $30 million dollars worth of t-shirts a year in fact.

Now, you may or may not have heard of Threadless, but they have the most amazing business model. They don't employ any t-shirt designers; instead they've developed a community of passionate artists who upload their own designs. The community then votes on the designs and the most popular ones get made into t-shirts, which you can buy for around $18.

Interestingly, when the concept was first established, the winning designers were paid $100, and they were delighted with that, which is a reminder that for some people, recognition is more important than money. Having said that, the winning prize amount has now gone up to a whopping $2500!

This type of customer community, or crowd-sourcing as some people refer to it, is a revolution in business.

Think about what's happening here. Customers are designing the products, acting as a sales force, and they're still customers because they're also buying the products!

How to Use This Lesson In Your Business

Think about ways to involve customers beyond what you're doing now.

Can you provide a way for them to submit their ideas, and reward them for doing so?

Is there some way to have them create new products using their own creativity and imagination?

Then, you can call on your customer community to vote on who has the best submissions. If a t-shirt company can do it, then the principle can be applied to lots of other types of businesses, and it's happening right now.

Another example is Dell, the computer company. They're using this idea to solicit feedback about their products - asking users what can be improved. Check out www.IdeaStorm.com - that's the place where you can give Dell a piece of your mind!

Chapter 24

1&1

This big marketing lesson is from 1&1, the domain and hosting company.

Now, I've never used their service personally, so this is not an endorsement, but I can tell you that they're certainly smart marketers.

For years, they've been using a marketing concept I call 'the unfair comparison'. I've also heard it referred to as 'buying criteria'.

It's a technique that you'll often see used on the side of software boxes, but in this instance, it's used by 1&1 in their magazine ads.

On the next page take a look at the chart with three columns, and see if you can spot the marketing lesson.

Compare Domain Registrars

Domain	1and1	GoDaddy	Yahoo!
.com	$ 4.99 first year *,** no setup fee	$11.99	$9.95
.net	$ 4.99 first year *,** no setup fee	$14.99	$9.95
.org	$ 4.99 first year *,** no setup fee	$14.99	$9.95
.info	$ 0.99 first year *,** no setup fee	$10.69	$9.95
.biz	$ 8.99 per year no setup fee	$14.99	$9.95
.us	$ 8.99 per year no setup fee	$19.99	$9.95
Email	Free 2 GB	Free 1 GB	No Mail
Private Domain Registration**	Included	$9.99	$9.00
.ICANN Fee**	Included	$0.18	Included

The first column represents 1&1, the other two are competitors - Yahoo and GoDaddy.

On each row are a variety of "buying criteria" that 1&1 wants us to consider, and they 'helpfully' show us how they and their competitors stack up on each feature.

Interestingly, all the products offered by 1&1 are highlighted in different colors, too.

Why is the chart laid out in this way?

Well, obviously 1&1 set the rules here. They decided what the buying criteria should be, and they've included points that are unique to their company!

With price they genuinely have an advantage, so they've made that much larger to make it stand out. But with some of the other points, it's really unclear what they mean, or how it would be an advantage. That's okay, because few people read through all the details - they tend to scan the chart. Note that point, it's important.

How to Use This Lesson In Your Business

You can use a chart like this in your business to highlight the buying criteria you want potential customers to consider, and give yourself an unfair advantage as a result.

First, think about the aspects of your business that are unique. You'll be highlighting those – the elements that you have that your competitors don't. Obviously, you need to make sure you get your facts straight when highlighting the weaknesses of your competition, but this type of weighted comparison can be a useful tool because it's so persuasive.

You're basically saying 'hey, no need to shop around - we've done that for you, and here's why we're the best choice.'

Let me know how you get on with implementing this in your business. You can email me at andrew@helpmybusiness.com

Chapter 25

Bose

This big marketing lesson is from Bose, the consumer audio company. I really like their noise cancelling headphones, although I'm not so keen on their other products. Some people say that Bose stands for **B**uy **O**ther **S**ound **E**quipment, and frankly I can see where that criticism stems from - I do think a lot of their products are overpriced; however, today we're looking at their marketing, rather than reviewing their audio quality.

Bose are masters of marketing, that's for sure. Just one example is how easy they make it for customers to refer a friend. In every set of headphones they place a few cards 'for your convenience.' So when someone says, "do you like those headphones", you can hand them the card with all the details of where they can buy a set for themselves. The card says:

"Customers tell us they're often asked about their Bose Quiet Comfort headphones. For your convenience, this courtesy card is yours to pass along".

It's a very simple idea, but very few businesses do this.

On the reverse side, it has contact details - phone numbers and websites for ten different countries.

How to Use This Lesson In Your Business

Could you include a simple card like that with your product, to make it easy for your customer to recommend it to someone else?

Taking the idea a stage further, could you personalize the card so you can reward the person who recommends your product or service? It could be as simple as leaving a space for the recommender to write their name and email address, so that they can be awarded a gift later on.

This is a marketing strategy that's virtually insignificant in cost, yet could easily bring you many new customers.

How many times have you asked someone where they bought an item, only for them to say, 'you know, I don't remember!' With this card, that won't happen anymore!

By the way, I mentioned VistaPrint in an earlier chapter - they're a very convenient resource for creating these type of cards.

Chapter 26

FIVE GUYS®
FAMOUS
BURGERS and FRIES

5 Guys

This big marketing lesson is from a fast food chain called 'Five Guys'. They recently opened a few stores near where I live in Utah, and I hear they're also popular in other areas of the States. The big lesson they provide is something that any business can do, yet most don't.

The reason I decided to try 5 Guys in the first place was because of the high profile media reviews (aka testimonials) that they feature in virtually all their promotions. You'll read sound-bite style comments such as "Best burger", "Best restaurant", "Best bargain", and so on - all from credible sources, and I took note of those endorsements.

Without reading those high profile comments, it's unlikely that I would have tried 5 Guys so urgently or enthusiastically. But I can tell you that in my region, their little restaurants are busier than a centipede at a toe counting contest!

It's sad that few businesses collect testimonials (comments from customers), let alone use them.

How to Use This Lesson In Your Business

Remember this: *what others say about you, your business, and your products, is a thousand times more persuasive than anything you tell them.* That's a fact of life. We'll listen to a third party much more closely than we will a salesman at the company. Again, what other customers say, counts far more than any claims a business owner makes directly.

Every piece of marketing that you produce must include positive, persuasive comments from other customers. Make that a rule. Add it to your business systems. So important is it, that I urge you to write it out a hundred times after you've finished this chapter, "I must include testimonials, I must include testimonials."

Do it, and your sales will increase!

Chapter 27

Nintendo

You may have heard of a little game console called the Nintendo Wii - it's the one that has the controller that you hold in your hand while moving it around energetically - with your body following along behind, trying to keep up. I hear that plenty of TV sets have been destroyed by people letting go of the controller, only to see it hurtle through the air and lodge itself in the middle of the screen, much to the users' horror and dismay.

There are some fantastic technical innovations in the Wii, but as we know, business is not about who has the best quality or cleverest product. What counts is the marketing.

Nintendo did something that isn't often talked about. It's the principle of scarcity - nothing to do with Halloween - that's scare-y, not scarci-ty!

Scarcity is where you deliberately limit the supply of a product or service, even when the demand is high. This plays on human psychology. If we can't have something, we tend to want it even more.

So, even after the Wii had been around for several years, it was still out of stock in most major U.S. stores. Whenever it came back into stock again, the built-up demand made it sell out almost immediately. In fact, some people were even camping outside their local Walmart or Best Buy store overnight when they heard about a new delivery coming in.

How to Use This Lesson In Your Business

How can you use this principle of scarcity in your business? You might try limiting the availability of a product or service. For example, a ski instructor might say:

"I only have six places for new clients, and four of those are already taken."

That's scarcity of quantity. And it's very legitimate and real.

There's also scarcity of time. An example would be where a store displays the sign: 'last day of sale.' That's scarcity, because the lower prices won't be available tomorrow. A time limit forces people to make a decision, because they know that if they procrastinate or put off the decision they could lose out.

Think about how you might use this concept of scarcity in your business, it's a powerful strategy.

Chapter 28

ORECK

Oreck

This big marketing lesson is from Oreck, the vacuum cleaner company. They've come up with a unique way to stand out in a crowded marketplace, and it works extremely well.

What's the secret? Quite simply, they offer a thirty-day, risk free trial. Anyone can buy one of their products, try it at home for thirty days, and if it doesn't work to their satisfaction, they can send it back for free.

That offer is central to Oreck's entire marketing plan and it works like a charm because it diffuses the objection of 'what if I don't like it?' That's an obvious potential barrier to a sale, so Oreck have eliminated it. Effectively, they're saying, 'We'll take the risk."

Take a look at their website at www.Oreck.com and you can see what I mean. The thirty day promise is clearly explained in three steps, with a personal message from the founder David Oreck.

I've included it on the next page for you to review.

Here's how it works: Take the Oreck Challenge® and try any Oreck product risk-free for 30 days. Then decide; **If you don't love it, you don't keep it®**. No obligation. Simply send it back, no questions asked — you pay no return shipping costs.— *David Oreck, Founder*

1.   **Purchase an Oreck.**

Shop online, find an Oreck Store near you, or call 1-800-219-2044 . Then buy an Oreck product.

2.   **Try it in your own home, on your toughest cleaning problems.**

Whether it's pet hair in your carpet or dust in the air, Oreck products tackle any cleaning problem with ease — thanks to innovative technology and superior engineering.

3.   **If you're not completely satisfied, return the Oreck product for a full refund.**

So how can you use this idea in your business? Well, before you get carried away, are you confident that your product or service is outstanding? Will it wow customers, as it should? If not, then your first priority before offering a trial period is to improve it. If you are confident in what you offer, stand behind that confidence with a thirty-day trial!

As another example, look at what I promise in offering my H3 lead generation course for eBay. I say:

"If after evaluating the system for up to thirty days you decide that it's not for you, send it back and you owe us nothing."

Implementing that risk-free trial period greatly increased sales. Yes, it also increased the number of people that took advantage of me in using it then returning it, but on balance the number of sales that stuck was still higher.

In the software world, it's very common to offer thirty-day trials where you can download some software and evaluate it risk-free.

Before they changed their model to the Creative Cloud program, Adobe used to offer all their software with a free 30 day trial period.

Again, this style of free trial works well because it eliminates the 'what if I don't like it?' barrier to buying.

How to Use This Lesson In Your Business

This is a simple one. If you can, offer some type of trial period for your products or services, especially if they skew towards premium prices.

Chapter 29

Rock Resorts

Rock Resorts is a luxury vacation company. Luci and I had booked a short stay in one of their resorts in Santa Fe and the booking process was very smooth. We found a place we liked, booked it online, and were sent a confirmation of the booking via email. That's fairly typical of how most hotel bookings are handled.

But with Rock resorts, it didn't end there. You see, about a week before we were due to arrive at the resort, we received a bulky package in the mail, and inside was a full color book about Santa Fe, showcasing the history, art, shopping, restaurants, and so on. This gift was completely unexpected of course, and as you might expect, it made us look forward to the trip even more.

How to Use This Lesson In Your Business

The lesson here is to ***surprise your customers with an occasional unexpected bonus.***

How many businesses do you know that send you a free gift out of the blue? These days you're lucky if you even get what you actually ordered!

So when you send something unexpected to your customers, you'll get noticed, you'll stand out from the crowd, and people will talk about you in a positive way.

By the way, the item doesn't have to cost a lot. In this example, the book actually didn't cost Rock Resorts anything - they acquire them free from their local chamber of commerce - their only expense is the envelope and postage.

What could you send as an unexpected bonus? Find something, try it for about a month, and then gauge the response, perhaps with a simple survey.

If it worked, implement it as a regular feature of your marketing systems so it doesn't get forgotten about. Remember, everything you do is marketing, and marketing is everything, and this is a classic example of that.

Incidentally, if you're already doing something like this in your business, let me know about it by sending an email to andrew@helpmybusiness.com

Chapter 30

B&H Photo Video

B&H Photo Video is a New York based distributor of all things audio-visual. If you're into gadgets and you haven't visited their superstore, it's definitely recommended. People visit from all over the world because they have just about every kind of consumer and professional electronics on display and in stock at competitive prices - cameras, camcorders, computers, recording equipment, lighting, you name it they have it.

Apart from being the biggest player in the consumer electronics field, B&H also separates themselves from the crowd by focusing on *helping* customers, rather than just trying to sell a large volume of products. One of the ways they do this is by having *knowledgeable* staff on hand. You can ask a question of anyone on the shop floor and they'll give you a helpful, intelligent answer based on actual knowledge of the products - try doing *that* at the big box stores.

B&H also make a variety of printed guides available free of charge, on helpful topics such as how to choose a camcorder and worldwide video standards.

How to Use This Lesson In Your Business

First, realize that it's frustrating for customers to ask a question and not be able to find any staff who know the answer. It's important to *have knowledgeable and helpful staff available to answer questions,* regardless of whether you have a physical store or operate online.

Secondly, help your customers by offering some *friendly, printed or downloadable information guides* that help them through the maze of product selection, as well as the buying process in your industry.

It might sound simple, but again, people don't buy just for the sake of buying - fundamentally, they are looking for help in solving a problem, so if you can *assist* them, you'll have their attention. They'll be more inclined to buy from you when you dont pressure them with hard-sell tactics.

Chapter 31

Siemens

Siemens, the electronics company is the subject of this BIG marketing lesson.

I know it's not the most glamorous company but among their zillions of products, Siemens manufacture an advanced hearing aid.

In terms of marketing, what does a company name a hearing aid? The 'Can you hear me now 2000'? The Deaf Defier 420'? The 'this one goes up to 11?' It's tough coming up with a name that stands out from the crowd and that isn't boring.

Siemens did something very smart; they created a name that provides a direct link with another well-known product - the Concorde. They called their hearing aid the 'Concordia DZII'. The important word here is Concordia, which is obviously deliberately designed to create a positive association.

Look, they even show a picture of a Concorde in their ad:

Most people subconsciously think 'speed of sound' when they think of Concorde, so you can start to understand why Siemens chose that name.

How to Use This Lesson In Your Business

Fundamentally we're talking about celebrity association here. Just as Siemens used Concorde to lend credibility to their hearing aid product, you can also **use celebrity association**.

The celebrity could be a product, or a person, and they don't even have to be directly employed by your company in order to gain benefit. For example, if you're in the business of selling sunglasses you might advertise a particular model as being worn by the Hollywood actors Tom Cruise and Brad Pitt. Do you get the idea here?

If you're marketing water, you might show a picture of an arctic glacier on the bottle, even if your bottling plant is in New Jersey. If you sell tea, you might quote a celebrity who says how much they love tea.

Here's an example from a local drama group in Utah. They create quirky comedy musicals based on well-known movies.

Some of their past shows have included 'Home School Musical', 'American Fork Idol', James Blonde, Snooty and the Beast, GhostBlasters, Grease'd, and so on. They've borrowed well-known titles and put their own twist on them:

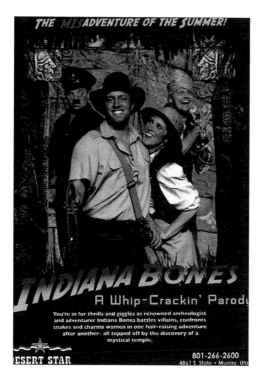

A word of caution before you get too carried away - always check with a lawyer before doing any kind of celebrity association. Even if you're not directly linking the celebrity to your product, it's wise to check to see if there are any implications you're not aware of. Still, don't be put off by the need to check with a lawyer. Businesses use celebrities in this way all the time, and you can too.

Incidentally, if you'd like to contact a celebrity to get an official endorsement for your product or service, (it's usually cheaper than you think by the way), go to **www.ContactAnyCelebrity.com** - it's the number one way to contact celebrities, and they offer a thirty day free-trial of their service. I've used their service in the past, and the results were good, so I recommend this service without hesitation.

Chapter 32

FedEx ®

Express

This big marketing lesson is from FedEx, the overnight shipping company. Although I'm actually a fan of FedEx, I believe they've done something very silly recently, and I'd love to get your thoughts on this. You might be aware that FedEx bought Kinkos back in 2004, they changed the name to FedEx Kinkos, and they've since invested in stores across the country.

Actually, Kinkos is such a well-established business that FedEx were willing to spend 2.4 billion dollars on the acquisition - so there's no doubt that Kinkos is a household name with a very strong brand that makes people instantly think copy and printing services.

FedEx in their infinite wisdom decided to drop the Kinkos name, and rename the stores 'FedEx Office'. Yes, I know, FedEx IS also a strong brand name, but when you think of FedEx, you don't think of printing and copying, you think of shipping. FedEx Office sounds like...a FedEx Office; it doesn't say what it really is. Not to mention the millions of dollars that'll be wrapped up in changing signage and all that kind of thing at all the stores. Actually, do you want to know the figure? FedEx shared it recently and the cost to change the name is $891 million dollars!

How to Use This Lesson In Your Business

Avoid messing with a proven formula. As entrepreneurs we often tend to get itchy feet - we get bored with consistency - we always want something new. But messing with something that's proven can have negative results.

So before you change your name, your USP (unique selling proposition), or anything else that's well established in your business, think carefully about the potential consequences, it might not be the best move.

Chapter 33

Du

Do you know Du? You Du? Well, if you don't, they're one of the most popular cell phone operators in the United Arab Emirates – I came across them for the first time on my recent trip to Dubai. Obviously I needed to be able to use my mobile without being charged $18 a second by my U.S. provider, so a couple of locals in Dubai told me that I should use Du. "Du you use Du?" I said. "We do use Du" they replied.

Well, I didn't expect too much when I went into the Du store, but by the time I left I was very impressed.

First, they had a specific solution for my needs as a visitor. I could buy a SIM card for my existing phone with some prepaid credit on it, in one easy package. Now, phone service isn't really an interesting product, is it? A SIM card isn't exactly the most exciting item in the world, and you can't *see* phone calls can you? Well, Du is the only cell phone company I've ever come across that realizes this, and they wowed me.

They presented me with an attractive, well designed box, and inside, in addition to the SIM card was a leather wallet. Inside the wallet, there's a visitor's guide to the region, cards to pass out that have your new number on them, tourist maps, a place for your passport and tickets, and even space for other credit cards. The best part was something so simple yet so important. Down at the bottom there's a place to store either your home SIM card, or the Du SIM card – what a great idea!

How to Use This Lesson In Your Business

The key lesson here is for the type of business that sells a service or a product that you can't see. When people can't see or touch what they're buying, they're often disappointed. So if you're in a service business, make sure that you over-deliver in designing something that the customer *can* see and touch. The Du wallet is an excellent example. It's not a requirement for the phone service to work, but it sets Du apart from the other providers, because the customer is 'wowed' when they first sign up for their service.

Think about what you can add as a physical product to your business, and if you're already doing it, share that with me by sending an email to andrew@helpmybusiness.com - I'd love to hear about it.

Chapter 34

McDonald's

Here's another big marketing lesson is from McDonald's. Whether or not you like the food, McDonald's definitely knows a thing or two about marketing. Actually they are experts at it which is why their business has grown faster than a wedding reception guest list.

The marketing lesson I want to show you today is something you don't see many business's doing. But it's a great way to increase profits, especially during tough economic times.

The picture from the McDonald's menu board explains the concept. What it's saying is if you decide to order a McRib you can add another one for just one dollar. Now obviously this is an irresistible offer that increases the overall profit on the sale. It works on the principle that it's better to make some profit rather than none. And essentially it's a specific type of up sell that combines the same product.

Here are some other examples - at this golf range you can buy one bucket of balls and get another at half price:

Buy One Get One Small Bucket of Balls
Parkside Driving Range & Batting Cages
Buy 1 small bucket of balls and get 1 free.
Offer Location: 68 Red Mills Rd, Pine Bush, NY
One coupon per customer per day.

At Lamas beauty you can buy one moisturizer and get a second for half price.

And there was an auto dealer that offered a deal where if you bought a Chrysler Pacifica they let you have a PT Cruiser for one dollar. One Dollar!

Here's a press release they put out about the offer:

Get The Chrysler Pacifica and get a second car, a PT Cruiser, for $1.

Frank Mancari started the deal on Saturday as a way to get people calling, booking appointments and visiting his Oak Lawn car lot at a time when many car dealerships are struggling to draw in customers.

"It's a once in a lifetime opportunity," Mancari said today, with an enthusiasm only a car salesman can muster. "There's no secret: the industry is slow right now. We're trying to generate activity with a great deal."

It works like this: Mancari said he wants to move the 2008 Pacificas off his lot. Those in stock are priced at $37,000 to $40,000, he said. The vehicles are larger, SUV-style, family luxury cars, he said. The PT Cruiser is also new but has low-mileage, and would give the buyer a more economical vehicle too.

"It's a great deal," Mancari said. "These are two great cars." Mancari has 5 Pacificas on his lot. Once they are all sold, the offer ends.

How to Use This Lesson In Your Business

Look for ways that you can offer this type of deal in your business. Many customers seek out bargains, so give them the opportunity to get extra value in their purchase while you also increase your profits.

Chapter 35

Netflix

This big marketing lesson is from Netflix, the popular DVD rental and online movie streaming service. Netflix sent me an envelope recently, and it turned out to be a very clever marketing piece because it looks exactly like the sleeve they use to send their DVD's in.

So at first glance, you think another DVD has arrived. But inside, there's an offer. Look how simply it's stated:

"You get free movies when your friends try Netflix."

This is a great headline because it gets right to the point with the key benefit highlighted in large letters. They also make it easy for the customer to get the benefit by including little cards that can be handed out to friends and family – so there's another lesson there.

The biggest lesson from Netflix with this example is simply to *offer an incentive to existing customers to get them to recommend the service to their friends.*

Can you see how brilliant that is? There is no better recommendation than word of mouth among friends, and Netflix have perfectly placed this promotion to capitalize on that.

How to Use This Lesson In Your Business

What could you do to get existing customers to recommend your products or services to their friends? The first step is to get their attention, then provide them with an irresistible incentive, (that's the 'what's in it for me') and finally make it easy for them to follow through.

Think about that over the next few days and let me know if you've come up with a way to implement this marketing technique in your business.

Chapter 36

Video Maker Magazine

This big marketing lesson is from VideoMaker magazine. When someone doesn't renew their subscription, one of the items they send out in the mail is this form:

Videomaker

Camcorders • Editing • Computer Video • Audio and Video Production • DVD

Two-Sided Story

Written by You and Me

MY SIDE **YOUR SIDE**

We hate to lose an old friend. The expression goes, "even your best friend won't tell you." But we are hoping that you will. Since we value your friendship, we are concerned that you haven't renewed your subscription to **Videomaker**. Perhaps it is our fault. We know you are busy, but if you could spare a minute, we would appreciate your help.

Have we let you down? Did you get your magazine on time, and was it in good shape? Maybe you wrote us about a question...did our answer help? We spend a lot of time on reader service, and you can help us judge if we're doing the kind of job we want to do.

If you have any ideas on improving **Videomaker**, we'd surely like to hear them. What do you like best? What don't you like? Are we just not meeting your needs? If so, why aren't we? Can we do anything to change

It's positioned as a 'two sided story' written by 'you and me.'

On the left hand side it starts with, 'We hate to lose an old friend' and then goes on to say things like, 'have we let you down? Did you get your magazine on time and in good shape?' Then further down in conclusion it says, 'so we're waiting to hear your side of the story.'

Now think about why the publisher does this. First, they don't want to lose any customers so this form is an effort to try and prevent that. Second, if someone is intent on leaving, they want to know why, so they can try and fix the problem for other customers in the future.

How to Use This Lesson In Your Business

The big lesson here should be obvious to you. Customers are valuable assets to every business. ***You should not want to let anyone go*** (unless they're being a gigantic pain in the posterior).

What system do you have in place to try and save customers? At the very least, do you always establish a way of finding out *why* they're unhappy? That information is incredibly useful to you, to help your business move forward with continual improvement.

If you don't have anything like this in place, write it down on your 'to do' list – it's crucial for your long-term success.

Chapter 37

Countrywide

This big marketing lesson is from Countrywide, the mortgage company, who are now defunct, as they were bought by Bank of America.

They really were one of the most incompetent companies that I've ever had the misfortune to be involved with. Let me explain…

I don't exaggerate when I tell you that they sent me at least one promotional mailing every week for more than a year and a half. After the first few weeks I gave them a call to see what they could offer me. They took some details, and no one ever called back. I called again a week or so later, the person I spoke to apologized, and said someone would call me back. Guess what? No one called back. I then contacted the company and asked them not to keep sending the mailers. Guess what? They continued to send the mailers until a few months before they went out of business.

Even if they had a deal to offer me, I wouldn't have been interested, because I was so irritated by their needless waste of money and resources.

How to Use This Lesson In Your Business

There are a couple of lessons here. First, *make sure you follow up with potential clients*, even if you can't offer them anything at that time. Simply not calling back is not an option. Who knows, they may have a friend who needs your service?

Another lesson is to *keep accurate records.* If someone asks to stop receiving information from you, honor that request. There's absolutely no value in sending marketing to someone that doesn't want it, is there?

When I send out emails to prospects and customers, occasionally someone will email me to say they don't want to receive any further correspondence. What do I do? Even though there's an easy to use link they can click at the bottom of the email that would instantly unsubscribe themselves, I do it for them. Look, I don't want anyone to receive information they don't want, its as simple as that.

So follow up, and keep accurate records in your business.

Remember, everything is marketing, and marketing is everything. If you irritate people, that's marketing! Countrywide irritated me to the point that I refused to do business with them - little did they realize that they were doing negative marketing.

Chapter 38

Pasqual's

This big marketing lesson is from Pasqual's restaurant in Santa Fe. It's not a 'big brand' per se, but they do provide a couple of lessons you can benefit from.

My parents were visiting recently so I took them down to Santa Fe, New Mexico, for a few days, and we stumbled across a restaurant called Pasqual's.

Now when I say 'stumbled across' let me explain what happened. We had no idea what restaurants were good because we'd never been to Santa Fe before, so we used my iPhone to look at a site called 'Yelp.com' which features independent restaurant reviews. We discovered Pasqual's, the reviews were great, and so we made a reservation.

Now, that's the first lesson.

If there's a website that features reviews for your line of business, make sure you're listed on there. If you're in the hotel business you want to be on TripAdvisor.com.

If you're in the electronics business you want to be on www.resellerratings.com.

If you're a builder in the U.S. you want to be on www.AngiesList.com or www.ThumbTack.com. In the UK you want to be on www.FindABuilder.co.uk.

Many industries have sites that can help you get your business noticed, and the better experience you deliver, the more prominent your company will be.

Now, back to Pasqual's. I talk a lot on my WebTV show (**www.HelpMyBusiness.com**) about creating an experience, and that's exactly what this restaurant does. One simple way they stand out from the crowd is to ***print their menu each day***, like this one.

Dinner

NAPO'S PUPUSA ~ Griddled Corn Masa Cake with Green Chile, Zucchini, Corn, Jack Cheese and Poblanos with Roasted Tomato Salsa and Salvadoran Escabeche 12

WARM FRENCH BRIE and Whole Head of Roasted Garlic with Salsas of Roasted Tomato~Jalapeño and Tomatillo 16

STEAMED PRINCE EDWARD ISLAND MUSSELS with Thai Basil, Lemongrass and Thai Chile Salsa, Grilled Garlic Bread and Chipotle Aioli Dipping Sauce 14 / 22

PAN SEARED CAPE COD SEA SCALLOPS with Orange~Saffron Butter, Sugar Snap Peas, Saffron Rice and a Haystack of Fried Leeks 29

CHICKEN PAILLARD with Brandy~Orange Marinade and Asparagus with Lemon Vinaigrette 26

Think about that. Customers feel extra special when they're told the menu is custom printed for that day, and regulars also find plenty of surprises to keep them coming back.

There are also benefits to the restaurant staff, too. Not only does it enable them to have every menu item up to date (none of the embarrassing 'I'm sorry we don't have that tonight Sir'), but it also allows them to try new dishes to see how they're received, plus they can vary the menu seasonally. In case you're wondering about the printing cost, it's just a simple piece of paper, printed with a laser printer!

How to Use This Lesson In Your Business

The lesson in your industry is to *challenge so called 'norms'*. Just because most restaurants have a fixed menu doesn't mean you have to do the same. Pasqual's stands out from the crowd with their custom daily printed menus. That kind of thing gets talked about a lot.

Sit down and make a list of every norm associated with your business, and look at ways to change some of those, to make the experience better. It's not that hard to do, it just requires a deliberate process.

Chapter 39

1-800-GOT-JUNK?®
THE WORLD'S LARGEST JUNK REMOVAL SERVICE

1-800-GotJunk

This big marketing lesson is from 1-800-GotJunk. Now here's a fascinating business. I talked with a couple of people recently who told me how impressed they were with this service. I asked why, and they told me a couple of things that were important to them. First, there was the speed of response. In both cases, they booked an appointment either by phone or online with the company in the morning, and someone was there in the afternoon. Second, the cleanliness of both the trucks and their staff was impressive. Third, the staff were friendly, courteous, and helpful. They arrived on time, and left the area looking clean and tidy.

It was interesting to me that neither person I spoke with mentioned the price. When I asked them about that, they both said something along the lines of, "well, I'm sure I could have got it cheaper, but I know there would have been a lot of hassles if I'd done that, and I'm delighted with the service of 1-800-GotJunk."

There are a number of lessons here for your business, but the one I want to hone in on is this matter of price.

Here's what you need to realize.

There are many people out there, even in a recession, for who *price is not their number one factor in making a buying decision.* More than anything else they want fast, efficient, and friendly service, with no hassle. That's what 1-800-GOTJUNK provides, and why not you too?

Let's look at the contrast in the junk removal industry. Taking the first USP of 1-800-GotJunk, that they're 'fast' – normally you'd probably place an ad on Craigslist, collect the responses, book someone whose reputation could well be dubious, and wait at home all afternoon because they can't guarantee that they'll be there at a specific time. How much time and money have you wasted right there?!

Then there's 'efficient'. The guy you booked on Craigslist shows up and says his normal truck broke down and he realizes that this truck isn't going to' be big enough for the job, so he'll come back the next day. Not too much of a stretch, is it?

Then there's 'friendly.' The Craigslist guy tells you that there's no way he's going to lift the heavy stuff, and he won't take some of it because that has to be taken to a different dumping area. Plus he tramps his dirty boots throughout the house, he borrows your phone because he doesn't have one, and he'll only accept cash. Again, not too much of a stretch to envision that situation, right?

Bearing in mind that time and hassle do have a monetary value attached to them, can you see why many smart people only want the best? It's because often it will actually work out cheaper in the long run to do that.

How to Use This Lesson In Your Business

The lesson in summary, is to ***avoid going after the lowest price point in your market***. Be the best. Offer the best service. Offer the best experience. Get people talking about how good your company is, you won't regret it.

Chapter 40

U-Haul

This big marketing lesson is from U-Haul, the truck rental company. I rented a truck from them a couple of weeks ago and when I came to sign the paperwork they showed me a laminated document that sent a chill through me.

It was a colored diagram of a truck with the scary headline:

'How will you be paying for damage?'

Below that headline the diagram listed all the things that I might knock, dent, scratch, lose, break-off, damage, or destroy.

$112 for a scratched decal, $419 for a damaged roof rail, and so on, and on.

It's a very clever marketing piece because *it instills fear.* It makes you think, 'what if I do damage the vehicle?' Suddenly, the cost of insurance looks very, very cheap compared to what you might have to pay if something goes wrong.

This is known as 'fear of loss' and it's a useful marketing principle to understand. While you don't want customers to be literally fearful, you sometimes want to remind them of the consequences of their actions.

106

How to Use This Lesson In Your Business

Let's give you some examples. If you're in the business of selling home alarm systems, you *could* promote a special offer price point as most do, but you'd be presuming that people were already convinced that they needed an alarm. A *better* strategy using 'fear of loss' would be to paint a picture of what can happen when you're home is broken into.

"Imagine the terror you'd feel waking up to see an intruder ransacking your home, emptying drawers, tearing up the furniture, and stealing your most prized possessions."

Get the idea? That's fear of loss.

Another example of this strategy would be for an item that's only available for a limited time. You could say something like,

"Once it's gone, it's gone. Think how disappointed you'd feel if you missed the boat on this never to be repeated item. We only have 32 remaining, and we'll never produce anymore like it."

That's another example of fear of loss. So in summary, remind the potential customer of the consequences of not buying, using, or re-ordering your product or service. It's a very powerful strategy. And yes, I did get the U-Haul insurance. Even I'm affected by fear of loss marketing!

Chapter 41

Lufthansa

This big marketing lesson is from Lufthansa, the German airline. Now, I have to admit, once in awhile those clever Germans come up with an idea that's really, really good, as in this example from Lufthansa. I was on a plane trip recently, thumbing through one of the in-flight magazines and I found this ticket:

Enter to win a Grand Prize luxury travel experience most people only dream about.

Take a virtual tour of Lufthansa at **www.lufthansa.com/moments**. Experience the airline with the highest standards in comfort and service in the air and on the ground and a network reaching to over 400 destinations worldwide from 22 North American gateways. When you fly Lufthansa, you will arrive at your destination on time, relaxed and ready for the day.

Luxury in the air and on the ground–the best of travel from Lufthansa.

Visit **www.lufthansa.com/moments** for the chance to win 2 First Class tickets to Munich and 5-star hotel accommodations at the Mandarin Oriental Munich. Plus, monthly prizes of 2 Business Class tickets and weekly prizes of Sennheiser headphones. To enter and for official rules visit **www.lufthansa.com/moments**.

Sweepstakes ends December 14, 2008.

Knowing how I would feel if I'd accidentally left a ticket on a plane, I was trying to think how I'd get it back to the rightful owner. Then, when I looked a bit more closely, I thought 'wait a minute' this isn't a ticket, it's advertising, and indeed it was.

The backside of the ticket explained that it was a promotion to win a luxury travel experience on Lufthansa.

The lesson here is to *use unconventional methods to grab the attention of your audience.* I'm sure you'd agree that most ads in most magazines get ignored. Why? Because, we've trained ourselves to tune them out most of the time. So by using this ticket in a magazine, it stands out, we notice it, it gets read, and if the offer appeals, we'll take action.

How to Use This Lesson In Your Business

In your business, *don't settle for using the traditional advertising media in the traditional way.* If all your competitors are in the newspaper in a certain section, why would you want to blend in with the crowd and bury your business somewhere in that 'heap'?

Be creative, and think of unusual ways to grab and keep the attention of your customers. If you get their attention, you've won half the battle, because that's the most difficult part.

Interestingly, I found another example of this type of strategy with an offer from American Express and Delta airlines. They sent this piece in the mail – and it looks exactly like a boarding pass, in a Delta sleeve.

You can see this piece on the next page…

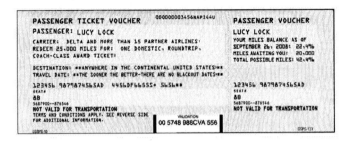

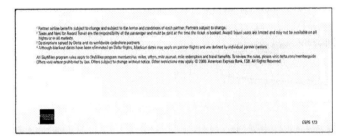

So this is going to get read, and like I said, that's half the battle.

So think about ways to get your business noticed. What unusual places could you advertise your business, or what unusual methods could you use?

Chapter 42

Old Navy

This BIG marketing lesson is from Old Navy, the clothing store. Luci received this package in the mail:

Look at the offer: "Get 20% off everything you stuff inside the bag when you use your gap card or banana republic card". There's also a specific date for the promotion.

I really like this concept because it engages the customer beyond just reading. There's something for them to do, to touch, and hold. It's also different, and even a little fun. The recipient probably thinks, 'hmm, how much can I cram in that bag?'

Then there's also a hidden agenda on the part of the company. Did you spot it? The promotion is only available to people who use their store credit card – so I suspect the real reason why they're sending this is to get lots more people to join that program, which in itself is a tremendous money maker.

How to Use This Lesson In Your Business

First, ***try and engage multiple senses of your potential customers*** – in this case they had something to read and interact with.

Second, if you want people to take an action that there's normally some resistance to, ***provide them with a compelling benefit***. In this case it was a 20% discount.

Last, ***make the promotion fun.*** It's not every day that you get an invitation to cram a bag with clothes and get 20% off the bill, is it?

112

Chapter 43

Dell

Dell, the computer manufacturer provides this big marketing lesson. I started to place an order for a new computer on their site recently, but I got distracted, so I didn't end up completing the order. The next day I had literally forgotten all about it, so I was very impressed when the next morning, I opened up my email and I saw a message from Dell. It was a friendly reminder to complete the order. I particularly like the wording they used. It said 'you're almost there' and reminded me that I had nearly placed the order, but not quite – no hard sell needed because I'd already chosen the computer, I just hadn't completed the order.

So the lesson for your business is to *have a process in place to manage the situation when someone doesn't complete an order.*

This is widely referred to as *shopping cart abandonment.* And as you can see from my example, there are lots of reasons why someone might not complete an order - never assume that it's because they didn't want the item. Obviously Dell have lots of resources at their disposal to implement the email system I just described, but it's not as complicated as you think, and of course it's important to remember the money you'll recoup on the orders that would otherwise have been abandoned.

If you have a physical store, rather than an online presence, how can YOU apply this principle? Well, just the other day I was at an audio equipment supplier and I was interested in a particular item, but I didn't know the price. So I took it up to the counter with the rest of my items and the price was a fair bit more than I'd anticipated. Seeing the look on my face, the salesman said,
"Let me see what I can do, you're a good customer of ours". He subsequently deducted about 20% off the price for me.

Now, the interesting thing about this was that it was still kind of high, it was more than I really wanted to pay, but because the salesman had made an effort for me and complimented me as a valued customer, I went ahead and bought the item.

So I thought that was an interesting example of how to resolve the situation of shopping cart abandonment in a real, bricks and mortar type business. I think you have to be careful with that, because you don't want customers to think that any price can be reduced if they just ask, but if you give a valid reason why the discount is given, the strategy can work well.

How to Use This Lesson In Your Business

Pay attention to customers that might be slipping through the cracks. If they've got to the stage where they've almost bought something, they're a hot prospect, and ultimately a valuable potential customer that you want to save.

Chapter 44

eBay

This BIG marketing lesson is from eBay. It's so simple that it's almost laughable, but many things in marketing are like that.

When someone reaches Power seller status as an eBay seller of a certain volume, they're sent a certificate.

It says 'in recognition of outstanding achievement' blah, blah, blah. Now, most people feel proud to receive this certificate. Looking at it one way (cynically), it's just a piece of paper, but to the recipient, its two important things. First, it's a pat on the back – 'well done'. Second, it gives a feeling of belonging. Those are two valuable things that leave a positive impression.

For the cost of a piece of paper and a stamp, eBay are making people happy, and they're much more likely to carry on selling, they'll feel more a part of the community, and their positive impression of eBay will increase.

How to Use This Lesson In Your Business

You need to *have a system in place to track your most valuable customers* – those that spend lots of money on your products or services.

115

Know who they are, and then ***reward them with unexpected bonuses***, a thank you card, and a gift, whatever - something!

Most business owners have no idea who their most valuable customers are, and unfortunately those customers end up getting treated no differently to anyone else, which is plain wrong – its bad for business. If you want these people to buy even *more* from you in the future, they deserve to be treated as special, singled out and acknowledged.

Chapter 45

DirecTV

This big marketing lesson is from DirecTV, the satellite TV provider.

They send out a newsletter with the bill that includes a one page, 'simple guide to understanding your bill.' It goes through each line of the bill to explain what everything means.

Why do you think they do this? Well, anytime you have a service that's comprised of various options or packages, it can be difficult for the customer to understand what the various charges are for.

DirecTV probably received lots of calls from customers who had questions about their bills, so this prevents many of those calls.

Remember, everything is marketing and marketing is everything. So what other underlying benefit is there here? Well, the company makes a positive impression because they're seen as trying to be open and transparent. After all, if there were hidden charges, they'd hardly dissect the bill in this way, would they? So this helpful guide makes the customer view DirecTV in an even more positive light.

117

How to Use This Lesson In Your Business

When there are common questions that seem to come up all the time, you can *cut down on support time by answering those questions up front, before they come up.*

For example, you might include an insert with each order; you might have a web page that answers questions, or some other way to communicate the details easily.

This kind of thoughtfulness improves the relationship with your customers, and cuts down work for your support staff.

Chapter 46

Entrepreneur®

Entrepreneur Magazine's
SmallBizBooks Division

This big marketing lesson is from Entrepreneur Magazine's SmallBizBooks division. They've produced a series of guides about how to start a business - but rather than going for a one size fits all approach, they offer a guide for each state in the U.S. So, it's 'How to start a business in Delaware', or whatever state you happen to live in.

Now then... although I haven't seen the guides personally, I'm pretty confident in saying that they're probably not completely different for each state. Most likely, they share many pages in common about general business tips, and they also include a section that contains specific information pertaining to the individual state.

From a marketing point of view, this is very smart. They could have offered one guide with all of the information on the various states compiled inside, but there's no way that would sell as well as the individual, more specific guides.

Basically, it comes down to buyer psychology. We buy products that closely match our needs. If we're starting a business in California and there's two guides offered – one is a general business startup guide, the other is 'how to start a business in

California' – which one will we go for? The California specific guide, every time.

How to Use This Lesson In Your Business

In your business, *try and match your products to the needs of your customers*, and do it in creative ways so that you don't recreate the work over and over again.

It reminds me of the printer who had a stack of business cards. If he met a lawyer, he would pull out a card that says 'specialist printer to lawyers'. If he met a doctor, he would grab a card that said, 'specialist printer to doctors' and so on. He knew that people gravitate towards specialists, and so he won tons of business with that simple, if cheeky strategy.

As another example, a friend of mine manufactured a product that killed all known household pests, but as a smart marketer, he realized that people don't shop for a product that kills all known household pests. Think about it – their house isn't being affected by *all* known household pests, is it? What people have is a specific problem – it could be mice, it could be roaches, it might be ants, or any one of countless other pests. People want to get rid of their specific problem.

So my friend made lots of new labels, poured the contents of the formula into new bottles, and offered, 'Mice Killer', 'Roach Killer', 'Ant Killer' and so on. What do you think happened to sales? That's right, they shot through the roof, because the product was perceived as a much closer match to the specific problem the person was having. So see if you can do a similar process in your business, by *naming products in a way that more closely matches the needs of your customers.*

120

Chapter 47

KFC

This big marketing lesson is from KFC –tthey wanted to be known as Kentucky Fried Chicken for awhile, but now they're back to KFC. Anyway, I digress. KFC has done a good job at tying their promotional campaigns into topical news, both nationally, and locally.

One example I came across was a double-sided flyer. On one side it said 'KFC Bailout Buckets' which was an obvious reference to the government bailouts that were going on at the time. Everyone was talking and thinking about bailouts, so KFC tapped into that with their promotion.

On the other side of the flyer, they presented a local tie in. In Salt Lake City where I live, they had opened up a new football stadium, and it said 'Great Deals for our Great Fans' with an offer to save money on tickets for the next game.

How to Use This Lesson In Your Business

In your business, ***can you tie in national news or well-known local events?*** It's important to stay informed and up to date with what's going on around you. Remember, these topics are on people's minds, they're being talked about at work, they're listening to the news on the radio or TV, or reading about it magazines or the newspaper. So when your marketing message ties in with that, it helps it to stand out from the crowd and be seen as more relevant and current.

If you have managed to tie news into your marketing, let me know about it by emailing me at andrew@helpmybusiness.com. I'd love to hear your story, and I know that other viewers of my show would too.

Chapter 48

Coca Cola

This big marketing lesson is from Coca Cola. If you've been to Disney World in recent years, you may have seen that Coca Cola now has a kind of outlet inside Epcot, where they let you taste some unusual country specific drinks manufactured by the Coca Cola company.

There's offerings from Israel (very tasty), Mexico (very tasty), Japan (absolutely disgusting) and Italy (my favorite!). I don't remember the names of the beverages, but they're all carbonated concoctions that were developed for the local population in each case.

Having the Coca Cola store and offering the unusual free drinks is a clever way for Coca Cola to interact with customers, but that's not the marketing lesson I wanted to share with you, it's something else that Coke is doing at the same outlet in Disney World.

They're offering both kids and adults the ability to 'Build a Cup'. If you're familiar with 'build-a-bear' stores, then 'build-a-cup' is just a variation on the same theme. And that's the point. The 'build a bear' idea is already proven, so the Coca Cola Company simply *borrowed an existing proven winner, put their own unique twist on it*, and came up with *Build-a-cup*.

You choose a colored cup, add some feet, add a hat and a straw, and so on, and the kids have lots of fun doing it.

How to Use This Lesson In Your Business

Are you on the lookout for proven concepts to adapt? As I've said before, it's not about directly *adopting* something that someone else has done, because every business has its own style. Rather, you need to *adapt what other successful businesses do, and implement your own variation of a proven idea.*

Stay on the lookout for good ideas to get a business noticed, then look at adapting them to suit your business.

124

Chapter 49

New York New York Hotel

New York New York hotel in Las Vegas provides this BIG marketing lesson. It's so good, they named it twice!

As you know, most hotels have a 'do not disturb' door hanger, as does New York New York. But some clever person in their marketing department apparently realized that it was unused marketing space, so now they use their door hangers to advertise their in-house Cirque du Soleil show, called Zumanity.

How to Use This Lesson In Your Business

Look for any missed opportunities to promote your business that you might have overlooked. In this example, the hotel already used door hangers, so adding the marketing message for the show didn't involve any significant expense. It was just unused space that lent itself to being used for promotion.

Think about items that your customers come into contact with – can some of them be used more effectively? A simple example is the delivery note that you send out with every physical order. You should be printing some kind of offer on that page. It might be a discount, a coupon, a buy this - get this free offer, and so on. There's no cost, because you're already sending a delivery note.

The same principle can be applied to customer emails. If you send customers an order acknowledgement, does it have a marketing message on it? The email being sent has the customer's attention, so you really should use that space to offer them something else.

Of course, there are limits on where to place a marketing message. For instance, not everyone agrees with ads in public bathrooms, like some I've seen!

Chapter 50

The Musician's Choice

Guitar Center

This big marketing lesson is from the Guitar Center, a popular chain of music stores here in the States. The company does a really good job of keeping in touch with their customers via direct mail – they send out catalogs, postcards, and recently a 'gift card' in the mail to all existing customers.

The promotion was a $10 gift card to use on anything in the store. Now there's some clever psychology going on here. The card was positioned as a $10 gift card *to be used like cash*, but if you think about it, it's really nothing more than a simple coupon. They could have simply printed a coupon for $10 off, and the end result would be the same. However, this way the perceived value of the card is so much higher than a coupon. Why is that? Well, no one would throw a gift card away, would they? But a printed coupon – they're everywhere; we see them all the time!

How to Use This Lesson In Your Business

Consider changing the way that you present offers. Coupons are good, but why not give out a gift card from time to time? Remember, customers will take notice of gift cards because they're rare, the perceived value is high, and the only cost to you is when someone redeems it for a purchase.

Ultimately, there's a powerful psychology when you 'burn a hole in somone's pocket with this strategy. If you 'give' someone some money (even in the form of a 'gift card'), they feel compelled to use it, rather than lose it.

In case you're wondering, these kinds of cards can be printed inexpensively by companies like ShortRunPlasticCards.com in the U.S. or PremierPlasticCards.co.uk in England.

Chapter 51

DinnerInTheSky.Com

This big marketing lesson is from www.DinnerInTheSky.com, a company that hosts dinners, literally in the sky. Here, take a look, it really is quite astonishing:

The table is about 150 feet high, suspended by a crane, and it holds up to twenty two diners. I'd try it, but I'd be afraid about asking for permission to leave the table!

129

Interestingly, this concept is actually quite simple. The creators built a sturdy platform with a dining table on it, and figured a way to make it completely safe for guests. When the dining table is full, they hoist it in the air with a crane, which is rented locally. Anyone could have come up with that idea, right? But they didn't, did they?!

Dinner in the Sky has received enormous attention in the media over the last few years, and for good reason – it's a very different, and unique dining experience.

How to Use This Lesson In Your Business

Think outside the box, creatively, to get noticed. That expression is almost a cliché, you've heard it many times before, but think about why it's so important to do that. It enables you to stand out from the crowd and also makes your job of marketing so much easier, because people will naturally want to tell others about it. So those are two important benefits that make it much easier to make money.

If your business is plain, even boring and dull, it's very difficult to get people to take notice of it, isn't it? I'm sure you've experienced that. But if you do something a little bit crazy, quirky, at the very least inject some personality into it, you're going to find it much easier to get customers, because people will choose to talk about your business.

Think about this. If I talked about five restaurants and 'Dinner in The Sky' was one of them, that would probably be the one you'd remember, because it's so different, right?

Don't settle for the easy route in your business because it'll actually be much harder to make money. Do something that gets people talking. Get noticed!

130

Chapter 52

amazon.com.

Amazon.com

This Big marketing lesson is from Amazon.com. Their eBook reader, the Kindle has become a big hit with people who enjoy reading. As part of their promotional efforts, Amazon did some creative advertising. A very clever ad appeared in *USA Today*, maybe you saw it at the time.

The ad said:

'In the time it takes you to skim the bestseller list, you can wirelessly download an entire book.'

There was an arrow in the middle of the ad pointing down to the USA Today books bestseller list below, which is a regular feature of the newspaper. So, Amazon was very strategic about *where* they placed the ad. They tied it in with the book bestseller list - because that's what their product is designed to do!

How to Use This Lesson In Your Business

The lesson for your business is to **think carefully about where you advertise.**

With some forethought, maybe you can tie in with an existing feature in a newspaper or magazine, or even website.

As an advanced technique, why not make your ad look like an editorial? In other words, use the same font and colors as the newspaper, magazine, or even website that you want it to appear in. That way, it'll look less like an ad, and more like editorial, a content piece.

The end result is that more people will take notice of what you have to say, and that's the point, isn't it?!

Chapter 53

FatCow Hosting

This BIG marketing lesson is from FatCow hosting, a name you may or may not be familiar with, but what a great name it is!

The company provides all kinds of web hosting services, which is not unusual, but what IS different is the way they've branded and promoted the company.

Going with the name FatCow has meant they can include lots of personality throughout the site. For example on the home page there's a reference to *'Fat Cow's Gone Free Range'*, the *'mini-moo'* lite option, and instead of a vision statement they've gone with a *'Heffer-Cratic Oath'!* And that's just on the front page! Elsewhere on the site, instead of describing hosting plans in the usual boring way, they've made it interesting and even entertaining, with the specs listed as *'Nutrition Facts.'*

Clearly, FatCow has done a great job at standing out from the crowd, or we might say ' the herd'!

133

How to Use This Lesson In Your Business

Inject personality into your company. Don't be afraid to let your hair down and use your imagination. The more unusual your branding is, the more likely that you'll get noticed. It's funny because from time to time stuffy, corporate types turn their noses up at branding like this, but you know what? It works!

If you want to blend in with everyone else, keep doing what you're doing, but if you want to get noticed (and get customers), inject some personality into your marketing and get noticed. That's what marketing should be!

Chapter 54

GoToMeeting®

GoToMeeting

GotoMeeting provides this big marketing lesson. I was on a flight recently and when my meal was served up, there was a little card on the tray, from GotoMeeting. The message said:

"Next time, try online meetings."

Now, this is quite smart if you think about it. The message was targeted at business travellers like me (because I was in first class). I *was* flying somewhere on business as were most of the others around me. And not only that, but the message was placed in front of me at a time when I was a captive audience. I wasn't distracted with work, so I had time to read the message on the card, which was brief.

How to Use This Lesson In Your Business

Try and make sure that your promotional efforts to use the right message, to reach the right customers, at the right time. Obviously there's no perfect way of doing this every time, but this was a good example of a campaign that was well thought out.

To use another example, suppose that you're a plumber. When you service a boiler or other appliance, you could place a sticker or magnet on the appliance, with a persuasive reason to call you

135

when it needs repair. Think how much extra business you'd get! Again, it's the right message to the right customer, at the right time. The message is carefully worded to reassure the customer that you're the best person for the job. The person reading it will be the right audience, and if the appliance goes wrong, they'll see the message at the right time.

How can you adapt this principle in your business?

Chapter 55

Fisher Wealth Management, LLC

Fisher Wealth Management

This big marketing lesson is from Fisher Wealth Management. Now, I can't endorse the company's services because I've never used them and I don't really know much about them, but I've been impressed with their marketing.

They sent me a letter, and I loved the simplicity of the message:

The headline at the top read:

"3 Reasons to read this letter"

...and then the 3 reasons given were:

1 – I'm not trying to sell you anything

2 – I am giving you something useful, for free

3 – My name is Ken Fisher, I am chairman of global money management firm Fisher Wealth Management and longstanding Forbes magazine columnist. People have been known to listen to what I have to say.

137

The positioning is very clever. Think about it. I wasn't expecting a letter from this company, in fact I'd never heard of them before - so there are two barriers in my mind – it's an unexpected letter from someone I don't know. It's obvious that whoever devised this mailing realized that would be a potential barrier, and they deliberately designed the opening few lines to overcome those objections.

They gave me not one, but three reasons to read the letter, and those reasons seemed fair, reasonable, and valid, didn't they?

How to Use This Lesson In Your Business

The principle to consider is all about *entering the conversation that's going on in the customer's own mind.*

You need to try and remove yourself from being a business owner to play the part of the customer, and do it regularly.

Try and look at your business through fresh eyes, as a customer. There's an old Chinese saying that 'there's no scenery in familiarity' and how true that is. When we're engrossed in our business, we often fail to see what customers see, and we can lose them through not being able to relate to them. So imagine yourself as your own customer, and then look for ways to better help your customers.

Chapter 56

Valenti

This big marketing lesson is from Valenti, a matchmaking firm, and when I say match making, I mean they don't make matches, they match make. I'm starting to confuse myself now. Anyway, this is an example of what not to do with your advertising. Here's a section of a full page ad that Valenti runs in all kinds of business magazines:

Obviously, you can't miss the fact that most of the page is taken up with a photo of the founder of the company, Miss Valenti herself. Now, the 'clever' wording that's far too clever for its own good is:

'The founders of Traditional Matchmaking'.

Now to me, those words mean nothing. It's a throwaway statement that elicits the response, 'who cares?' What is traditional matchmaking anyway, and do I really want traditional? And who cares if you were the founder? What are you going to do for me now?

Below the clever wording there's a logo, which again has no benefit attached to it whatsoever, and then down at the bottom, in the tiniest print, almost as an afterthought, the website domain name, and a phone number.

But why would we call them or visit their site? We haven't been given any reason to do that with their ad. This is called image advertising. It's basically saying, 'we're here, and we're really good.'

This kind of advertising is a complete waste of time and money. Think about it, there's no attention-grabbing headline, there's no compelling reason to look into the company further, there's no limited time offer, there's no instruction to the reader of any kind.

How to Use This Lesson In Your Business

This is a simple one. *Please* do not fall into the trap of creating image advertising that just exists. You must have a clear call to action to make every piece direct response.

Chapter 57

Rosetta Stone

Rosetta Stone language learning system has some great print ads.

Visualize the scene. We see a guy sitting in the corner of the room, clearly out of the loop and feeling like a dunce. The headline says:

"Ever felt a little left out on business trips abroad? Rosetta Stone will save your blushes".

Then, the next line continues:

"The fastest and easiest way to learn French, guaranteed."

So, if we're the right target demographic, we've been reminded of a painful situation that we face of not knowing the local language, and we've been given a solution. *The combination of problem with solution is the essence of good marketing.* First, state a common problem, and then provide the solution.

The blurb below that in the ad, lists all of the languages that are available, and then it goes into detail about what makes Rosetta Stone better than other language learning systems.

What other elements make this a good ad?

Well, there's an offer, namely to get 10% off by using a coupon code online.

There are two guarantees - first, a "No risk, six month money back guarantee". Then at the bottom, the companies USP is also, a guarantee, "The fastest way to learn a language, guaranteed."

There are also multiple ways to respond to the ad - you can phone, you can go online, or you can send in the coupon. This is great because people have different preferences. And it's important to note that fundamentally, this ad is designed for one purpose, to get people to respond. It tells the reader exactly what to do, so it's known as direct response.

Unfortunately most ads just tell the reader, 'we exist and we're really good' but they never instruct the reader to do anything, so the ads are wasted.

The colors are also good with this ad - notice how the yellow sections really stand out and grab your attention.

Now then, for all this ads great points, it still has one fatal flaw. Something is missing that would dramatically increase the effectiveness of this ad. It's the fact that there's no deadline, and therefore no urgency.

How to Use This Lesson In Your Business

Review your own ads, to make sure they include an offer, a guarantee, multiple ways to respond, and an attention-grabbing design.

Chapter 58

DirecTV

DirecTV is a leading satellite TV provider in the U.S.A. I came across one of their ads in Inc magazine recently, and it was an excellent example of how to broaden your customer base:

DirecTV are known for providing satellite TV service into homes, but look at who this ad is targeted to. It says:

"DirecTV turns your waiting room into an 'I don't mind waiting room"

So this message is designed to appeal to any business owner that has a waiting room - doctors, dentists, chiropractors, car repair shops, hair salons, and so on. The lesson here is that DirecTV asked themselves the question, "what other markets or demographics can use our service?"

How to Use This Lesson In Your Business

I'd like you to ask this question about your business: "Who *else* can use our service?"

There's one particularly great way to find the answer to that question? It's very simple. Ask your customers! Send them a survey, with a question like, "do you use any of our products or services in an unusual way, if so we'd love to hear about it."

As an example, although my WebTV show (www.HelpMyBusiness.com) is designed for entrepreneurs and small business owners, when I surveyed my viewers I discovered that the show is watched in some colleges and universities by students as part of their curriculum. Also, there are lots of viewers under the age of 15 who want to be entrepreneurs. I also found out that there are plenty of viewers of retirement age who enjoy learning.

The show wasn't aimed at any of those groups. But when I discovered that information, I made some subtle changes that were designed to acknowledge those audiences occasionally. Who uses your products? When? And How?

144

Chapter 59

Delta Airlines

This big marketing lesson is from Delta Airlines. I'm a regular flyer with Delta because they have a hub near where I live in Salt Lake City. I don't think they're particularly better or worse than most other airlines, but they did do something recently that impressed me, and that I wanted to share that with you.

They sent me a bunch of certificates, which are designed to recognize employees that go above and beyond the call of duty.

I put a few in my travel bag so I'd have them to hand, and on my very next trip I noted a flight attendant who was doing an outstanding job. She was warm and friendly, nothing was too much trouble, and she had a great attitude. She really made the journey more enjoyable for me, so I whipped out a certificate, filled in a few details and at the end of the flight I handed it to her. Not only did her face light up and she thanked me profusely, but also I felt really good about giving the reward.

I was thinking about that experience and I realized that there's more to this concept than I initially realized. You see, when I first stowed those certificates in my bag, on my next flight I began to look for the good, the positive, and the outstanding achievements. I was focused on finding all the good things. Interesting, isn't it?

How to Use This Lesson In Your Business

I'd like you to think about the principle here of ***helping your customers notice the good things you do.*** It may not be practical to come up with a system of certificates, but you can definitely encourage customers to let you know when one of your employees goes the extra mile.

The employee needs to be rewarded for that. Also, realize that customers feel good about giving a reward, too. It'll help them stay loyal to your company!

Chapter 60

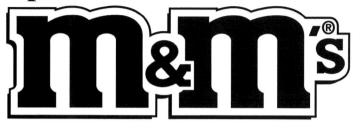

M&M's Candy

This big marketing lesson is from M&M's candy, or 'sweets' as we Brit's like to say.

From time to time you'll see a limited edition flavor of M&M's like these, the coconut flavor. Very Delish!

The point of this is a proven marketing concept with two key benefits: interaction and the opportunity to do a risk-free test.

147

How to Use This Lesson In Your Business

First, keep customers enthusiastic about your product by introducing new variations of something they already like.

Second, know that you can test a product in the marketplace to gauge the response. If people love it or hate it, it will soon be obvious. And if it doesn't work out, they haven't really lost anything because it was positioned as a limited edition.

In your business, can you create some limited edition products either to offer a variation in the marketplace, or simply as a marketing test?

Chapter 61

TGI Friday's

This big marketing lesson is from TGI Friday's. I was in the restaurant a few days ago with an acquaintance, and when we were shown to our seats, the host placed a card and a pen on the table, she then explained the benefits of their loyalty scheme, and encouraged us to sign up:

Now, I was very impressed because she'd done something very important in those few seconds. Apart from having a loyalty scheme, which is an important lesson in itself, that host carried out

149

some specific, deliberate actions to make it as easy as possible for me to signup.

First, they brought the program to my attention by telling me about it as we sat down. Second, the timing was perfect because it was at the *start* of the meal when we could give it our attention (while we waited for the food to arrive).

And third, she left a pen for me to fill in the form. Again, she realized that not everyone would have a pen on them, and now there was no reason for me NOT to fill in the form. ***Every obstacle had been removed.***

How to Use This Lesson In Your Business

The first key lesson here for your business is, *don't assume that customers know about your loyalty program, special offers, or any other interesting things that you're doing in your business.* Most of the time, they don't.

Also, if you want customers to take a specific action, such as joining a loyalty program, make it as easy as possible for them to do it. Remove all the potential obstacles or excuses. Like I said, I was impressed with TGI Friday's, and yes I did fill in the form!

Chapter 62

Masterplans.com

This big marketing lesson is from Masterplans.com, a company that helps you create a business plan. I saw one of their ads in Entrepreneur magazine, and there's something very persuasive about it that most people would miss.

It's nothing visual; in fact it's the choice of words. The headline asks a question:

Need funding for your business?

Then at the bottom, it says:

You need master plans.

The reason this is a good piece of copywriting is because it shows an understanding of what the customer really wants - the *end* benefit of using their product.

This concept can take awhile to get your head around, so I'll try and explain it further.

What you would *expect* to see in an ad like this, is something like the following headline:

Master plans is the #1 way to help you write a business plan.

The problem with that statement is that it doesn't speak to what the customer *really* wants or needs, deep down. To the customer, it's really not about writing a business plan, it's about being able to get a new business off the ground successfully, or perhaps find a source of funding. See the difference?

How to Use This Lesson In Your Business

In your ads, try and drill down much deeper than your competitors do, to really ***understand the end result that the customer wants.***

To give you another example, if you were advertising a new kind of shampoo, the purpose of that product is obviously to keep your hair clean, right? Factually that's true, but that's not the real reason why most people buy shampoo. The deeper reason, the end result, is that they want to feel or look more attractive as a result. In other words, there's an underlying reason *why* people want to wash their hair.

Study this concept and you'll see that the most effective ads typically focus on the *ultimate* benefit, rather than the most obvious one. It's a more advanced concept to understand and implement, but you can handle it! I'd love to hear how you reposition your product or service in a more effective way. You can email me at andrew@helpmybusiness.com.

152

Chapter 63

Jamba Juice

This big marketing lesson is from Jamba Juice, a well-known U.S. based chain of juicing stores, serving all kinds of blended juices and smoothies.

Jamba Juice opened up another market for themselves in certain regions by offering a delivery service. Why is that a good idea? Well, since all their juices are made fresh to order, at certain times of the day it can get really busy in the stores, which can lead to a long wait. Now, in certain areas you can simply fax your order in, and it'll be ready to pickup, or it can be delivered at your convenience. Everyone's happy!

One of my cousins setup a successful sandwich delivery service in her hometown in England. The region had lots of small industrial units, with very few places to get lunch. She setup several vans that delivered food during the morning, before lunchtime, and took the food directly to the workers. Interestingly, in the town there are lots of cafes and restaurants, and any one of them could have done the same thing, but they didn't think of it.

153

Strategically, think about where your customers are hanging out. Where are they grouped together conveniently for you to take your product or service directly to them?

How to Use This Lesson In Your Business

Look for ways to expand the reach of your products or services.

If you don't currently offer delivery, could you? If you only offer delivery, could you setup a store location for people who want to come to you?   Don't be limited by the way you currently do business. Challenge every so-called 'norm' in your industry and look for better ways of reaching those who want to buy from you.

154

Chapter 64

Hyatt Hotels

This week's big marketing lesson is from Hyatt hotels. A friend of mine, Jason Van Orden was staying at the Hyatt hotel in Austin, and he was surprised to receive a Tweet from the hotel concierge. It said:

> 'Welcome to Hyatt! Need fun ideas for tonight?
> Enjoy the conference!'

How did they know that Jason was staying there? Quite simply, they had seen one of his tweets where he mentioned the Hyatt.

Now think about what the hotel did there.

They engaged with some of their guests using a communication medium that some of their guests enjoy using, namely Twitter. And the exact same thing could be done with other social media platforms like Facebook or Instagram.

How to Use This Lesson In Your Business

The lesson here is to *look for creative ways to engage with your customers.*

Remember, other media like email is often less effective these days because there's so much clutter, junk, and spam out there. It's tough to break through that and stand out from the crowd. So even if you're not a big fan of social media, realize that many people are, and you're wise to embrace it as a business tool, rather than reject it because you don't like it or understand it.

The specific tools such as Twitter, Instagram, Pinterest, and Facebook will likely change over time (remember MySpace?), but social media is here to stay.

Chapter 65

jetBlue
AIRWAYS®

JetBlue

This big marketing lesson is from JetBlue, the American based airline. You might have seen an offer where JetBlue offered an 'all you can jet' pass for $599. It was valid for a month, and it allowed you to travel anywhere on their 50 city nationwide network.

I loved this offer, I thought it was brilliant marketing, and sure enough, it sold out within days of going on sale. In fact, hits on JetBlue's website skyrocketed by 700% in the days after the promotion was announced. Interestingly, I've never seen any other airline make that kind of offer. Remember, airlines are a hugely competitive business, and the offer appeared during September, traditionally a slow time of year for airlines. So JetBlue really broke the mold about how flights are sold, and came up with an irresistible offer.

How to Use This Lesson In Your Business

The lesson for your business is to *challenge the existing pricing model and look for new, creative ways to sell your product or service.*

For example, if your industry traditionally charges by the hour, what's to stop you offering a monthly membership instead? Or if

157

everyone in your industry charges an annual fee, could you scrap that and make the money back in another area instead?

Could you follow JetBlue's idea and create an 'all you can consume' offer for a week, a month, or even a year? The point is, when you offer something radically different from your competitors, you get noticed, you get talked about, and invariably you get more sales!

Chapter 66

Liberty Mutual Insurance Company

This big marketing lesson is from Liberty Mutual Insurance Company. As a Home Depot credit card customer, I received a flyer in the mail along with my credit card statement from Home Depot.

The headline said:

> "As one of Home Depot's credit card holders, you could save hundreds of dollars a year on auto insurance."

Can you see what they've done here? Fellow marketing expert Mark Joyner calls this strategy 'Integration Marketing' and I think that's a really good term for it because Liberty Mutual are *integrating* their marketing message into *existing* communication from Home Depot. They saw a match, and they pay Home Depot to include these inserts into the statements of their cardholders.

Another example of Integration marketing is where Google offer their Internet browser toolbar at the time you install certain software. In other words, Google integrate that offer, so that it appears in front of someone else's customer. When someone does

159

install the toolbar, it's my understanding that Google pays the third party on a cost per action basis.

Ultimately, this kind of transaction is becoming more popular because both companies benefit. In the Google example, Google acquires a customer, and the software seller makes more money from the same number of customers, by including another offer from a third party that they've carefully screened, and trust.

The lesson here is to ***understand the importance and effectiveness of integration marketing,*** i.e. including an offer for your product or service in someone else's business.

Another example of this concept from big business is McDonald's. Often, when you order a burger, they'll ask you if you'd like to add a Coke. Coke is not a McDonald's product, but they integrate it into their own business seamlessly and effectively.

How to Use This Lesson In Your Business

The first step is to ask yourself, 'who else sells to my type of customers'?

If you're a dentist, you might get together with a chiropractor and when he or she sends their new patients a welcome letter, they could invite those customers to request a free first visit at the dentist. If you're a plumber, you could track down a friendly electrician and when the electrician leaves his card with a customer, he could leave your card too, with an offer for a "free home electrical safety survey".

This is a very powerful concept, and if you want to learn more about integration marketing, I encourage you to check out the website: www.IntegrationMarketing.com

160

Chapter 67

Dell

Here's a BIG marketing lesson from Dell computers. I received a flyer in the mail from them, and it was an invitation to their 'signature event'.

Inside the flyer, there was a special offer for each day of the week during the period of the event, and I was reminded that 'when it's gone, it's gone' – in other words, don't delay in ordering. I was also directed to a special website setup for the offer.

How to Use This Lesson In Your Business

The principle to learn here from Dell is to *create special events to make the buying process more appealing.*

An event is a special occasion that has a positive, even exciting connotation, so when you invite your customers to an event, they feel more valued. Why not schedule at least two or three events each year where you create a theme or an environment where you can make special offers for your customers. It could be a 'we're moving office' event; it might be a 'name your own price' opportunity, or perhaps like Dell, a different special offer each day over the period of a week. Again, this kind of event is very effective at boosting sales.

Chapter 68

Austin American Statesman

This big marketing lesson is from the *Austin American Statesman,* a popular newspaper in Austin, Texas.

I picked up a copy when I was in town, and I noticed a splash graphic on the front cover.

It said:

$167.60 in Coupons and Savings Inside Today's Paper.

Now this is a very useful marketing strategy. What they're doing here is reminding anyone that's reading or considering reading the paper, that they can save a lot of money. In fact, there's a specific dollar amount cited here. Subconsciously, the message that's conveyed in this graphic is, 'for an outlay of $1.60, you can get a potential return of $167.60'. It's reminding the reader about the value proposition that's on offer.

How to Use This Lesson In Your Business

Never assume that customers know or understand the true value of your product or service - you must tell them, and tell them explicitly. Spell it out.

For example, if you sell home insurance, you might compare the true cost of repairing minor flood damage to the measly monthly investment to be insured.

If you sell software, you could remind customers that automating a process using your software usually means you can free up seven hours each week to work on other things.

If you're an interior designer, you might tell customers that the discounts you've negotiated with leading industry suppliers will more than cover the price of your service.

All of those examples are persuasive, aren't they? And that's the point. So again, never assume that customers know or understand the true value of your product or service - remind them in an obvious way.

Chapter 69

Conde Nast

This big marketing lesson is from Conde Nast Portfolio magazine. They sent me an invitation to try a new magazine called 'Portfolio' and the interesting thing to note on the offer is that there were two reasons to respond.

First, I could get each issue for just a $1 - the cover price was significantly more, obviously. And secondly, I was also offered a USB flash drive, as a free gift. Those two elements combined made this a very persuasive offer.

How to Use This Lesson In Your Business

Provide two motivating and persuasive reasons to respond, when sending out an offer.

In infomercials, I'm sure you've noticed how they build the value of the offer gradually by adding other bonuses. This is very similar. You make an irresistible offer, and then *add* another free gift or some other compelling motivation as to why the person should respond. Instead of just one reason to respond, they now have two. Got it? Now, go put it into practice!

164

Chapter 70

Netflix

This is another big marketing lesson from Netflix. I've been a subscriber for a few years now, and I love their on-demand service where you can choose movies and TV shows to watch instantly. We have Netflix hooked up to a media center computer so we can watch shows on our TV. Anyway, recently there was a problem with the credit card on my account, so Netflix sent me an email. In the subject line it says:

'We're missing some info'

Then the main message says:

Dear Andrew, we're glad you're a Netflix customer, but we've had some trouble authorizing your MasterCard. To keep your movies coming, try this...

...and then they give some specific steps on what to do.

I'm sure you can tell already that this message isn't the typical approach that companies use when a charge gets declined. The wording that Netflix uses is so much friendlier than what you usually see. And that's the point here.

There are all kinds of reasons why someone's card declines - it could be expired, the customer might have moved address, there might be a security flag on it, and so on. So I really like the way that Netflix defuses the awkward situation by saying, We're missing some info' - see how much better that is than 'your card declined, pay up or we'll shut you off!' Sadly, that's the kind of message that most businesses use - maybe not those exact words, but that's the tone, isn't it?

How to Use This Lesson In Your Business

When a credit or debit card declines, don't make the customer feel bad. Apologize for the situation and you'll find that the customer is far more likely to want to continue doing business with you. On the other hand, if you point the finger at them and make them feel bad, it'll probably make them feel embarrassed and less likely to want to resolve the situation.

Chapter 71

ROM

This big marketing lesson is from the makers of ROM, a specialist fitness machine. You might have seen their ads in airline magazines or other high-end business magazines.

Compared with the average piece of fitness equipment, the ROM is expensive. Very expensive! As in, around $15,000!

The ad for ROM has been running for years, so clearly it's working. One of the reasons it's working is because they've targeted the right demographic - wealthy people who can afford it and who see the benefits attached to it.

That might seem like an obvious statement, but I see many businesses who advertise in the wrong places - places that aren't congruent to their business. For example, many bus stops seem to have ads for high-end jewelry or other luxury items - that doesn't make sense, does it?

I see ads in the yellow pages that target students. Well, when was the last time a student picked up the yellow pages? Generally, they don't, because most of them are online.

I've also seen ads on social networks like Facebook promoting hearing aids for elderly people! How many old grannies do you know that are hanging out on Facebook? Yes, there are a few, but it's not the most logical place to target that product. And yes, I know that not everyone who wears a hearing aid is old, but the demographic definitely skews older, that's the point.

How to Use This Lesson In Your Business

Give close attention to where you advertise. It matters. Always *make sure it's a good fit with your primary target audience, your main demographic.*

Chapter 72

Häagen Dazs

I was passing by a Häagen Dazs store when one of their employees standing out front handed me a money saving coupon.

Not only did that show initiative, but the coupon was made to look like a dollar bill.

People are magnetically attracted to money, we just can't help it, so there's an added psychological benefit. If someone handed you a real dollar bill you certainly wouldn't refuse it, and the same principle applies here.

How to Use This Lesson In Your Business

In your marketing, leverage the look of money. For example, if you offer $10 off, show a $10 note in your ad. If you're handing out coupons, make them look like money.

Of course, don't photocopy real money because that could get you into a lot of trouble, but Haagen Dazs was a great example of how to do it, they customized a bank note with their logo.

169

As another example, I created an elongated postcard that looked like a $20 bill for a promotion at a tradeshow. It said:

Turn over to discover how to grab your free gift (with a $20 value).

Again, leverage the psychology of how we view money in your marketing. And if you're an International reader, I apologize about the dollar example, but you get the point - just use your own currency; pounds, yen, rubels, rupee, dong, euro, or whatever applies.

Chapter 73

IHOP Restaurants

This big marketing lesson is from IHOP restaurants, or as I used to refer to them for the longest time: OneHOP (I saw 1HOP when I read the sign). No one told me, how was I supposed to know?!

Anyway, IHOP does a good job at creating special menus that tie in with popular interests. For example, a promotion with the NFL resulted in a special menu called the *"Hunger Strategy Playbook"*. Inside, choices included the *ADC Stuffed French toast* in the shape of a football, the *Touchdown Sampler*, and the *Quarterback Scramble*.

Now, in my opinion the link between NFL and IHOP is a bit of a stretch, I mean I can't imagine that any players eat there to be honest, but hey this is marketing, and it works! They've managed to make the menu fresh, dynamic, and appealing by simply theming it around a popular subject.

How to Use This Lesson In Your Business

How can you present your products more creatively? Can you come up with a popular theme to tie in to? Here's the point: *a product promoted around an already popular theme will always sell better than the 'plain vanilla' approach.*

Most marketing is boring, and the product gets lost in a sea of sameness.

This concept works with services too. In one of the early chapters of this book, I featured a dentist in Orlando who's branded his practice around a Star Trek and Star Wars theme. It's called "Starbase Dental," and it's so popular that they have to turn customers away.

You have to admit that being greeted with, "May the floss be with you" and then being invited to choose an episode to watch on a monitor by the chair is enormously helpful in overcoming the usual dread and anxiety associated with going to the dentist.

Don't be afraid to step outside your comfort zone and push the envelope with your business. Tying it in with a popular theme will get you noticed, it'll get you more customers, and those customers will usually be happier, too.

Chapter 74

Delta Airlines

This big marketing lesson is another from Delta Airlines.

Luci and I were on a flight that was delayed from Salt Lake City, and although it was irritating, we don't expect too much from any airline, other than perhaps Virgin and JetBlue. Anyway, a week or two after that incident, I received a letter from Delta not only apologizing for the delay, but they also gave us a gift of bonus miles, too. I've been delayed many times on many airlines and this is the first time I've ever received a letter like this.

Dear Mr. Lock:

Delta Air Lines would like to take this opportunity to apologize for the delay of Flight DL1157 on October 4, 2009.

In this competitive airline industry, travelers expect the best value for their travel dollar. The best value is a complicated mix of safety, on-time operations, courteous efficient service, as well as a wide range of destination options. Occasionally, we must compromise on-time operations to guarantee safe travel. Unfortunately, this was one of those times.

I personally want to apologize to you for the delay in your travel plans. To show you my commitment to quality service, I am adding 2500 bonus miles to your SkyMiles account 2482886708. Please visit us at nwa.com/skymiles or delta.com/skymiles to verify your mileage balance.

Loyal customers are key to any company's success, and it is our goal to provide excellent service on every occasion. I hope you will give us an opportunity to restore your confidence and to welcome you on Delta and our SkyTeam partners in the very near future.

Sincerely,

Elizabeth Reed

Elizabeth Reed
General Manager, Customer Care

I was really impressed with Delta for the way they handled this incident. I've told lots of people about it, including you, and what

173

has it cost them? Probably just a few dollars per customer who were delayed, to have a really positive effect.

How to Use This Lesson In Your Business

In your business, ***when things go wrong, proactively try and make it up to customers automatically, don't just react when someone complains.***

I think you can see from this example that the proactive approach is so much better. Not only do customers appreciate it, and you're likely to retain their business, but because so few companies care anymore, you'll also stand out from the crowd, which is exactly what most business are trying to do!

Chapter 75

Hotels.com

This big marketing lesson is from Hotels.com, a popular online hotel booking service.

There was a time when I used to belong to various hotel chain loyalty programs, and I resonated with the character played by George Clooney in the movie *Up In The Air,* as he compares his stack of loyalty cards with another frequent traveller.

Hilton Honors, Hyatt Gold Passport, Star Rewards - you name it, I belonged to it. And to be honest it was a hassle belonging to so many programs, because there's so many cards to carry, so many membership numbers to remember, and then there's all the points and rewards that have to be tracked.

The associated challenge was that I'm really not enough of a fan of a single hotel chain to give them all my business, and it probably wouldn't be practical to do that everywhere I travel anyway. I realized that I stay at many different hotels - whatever happens to be the best choice for the location, time of year, and other circumstances.

I was thrilled to discover the Hotels.com loyalty program. It's extraordinary. For every hotel night you book with them at any hotel costing more than $40 a night, after ten cumulative nights, you get a free night at any hotel for a future booking.

To give you an example, imagine that you booked three nights at a Hilton, and then the next month you book five nights at a Hyatt, and then later in the year you stay for two nights at a Holiday Inn. As soon as you've accumulated and completed those ten nights of bookings, you get a free night up to the value of the average cost of those ten nights.

I've given up all the other confusing hotel loyalty schemes and now I get a significant, practical, and regular reward with the ability to be completely flexible in which hotels I choose.

Keep in mind that the travel industry is fiercely competitive. You have companies like Priceline, Expedia, Travelocity and so on all trying to compete. Along came Hotels.com and they not only match or beat the prices of the other providers, but they also offer this great loyalty scheme that truly serves the customer. Personally, I don't book hotels at any other website now!

Can you see how important it is to separate your business from competitors by doing something completely different? None of the well-known websites I mentioned can compete on price alone, that's a losing battle that benefits no one. But they *can* listen to travelers and give them something that does have enormous value, as in this case with Hotels.com.

How to Use This Lesson In Your Business

What do customers really want? What do they complain about in your industry? If you can fix that problem and then spread the word, you'll win every time.

Chapter 76

WinCo FOODS

WinCo Foods

This big marketing lesson is from WinCo Foods, who operate Winco Supermarkets. They're a new player in the area where I live, and boy have they caused a stir. They've bulldozed their way into the marketplace with brand new stores and incredibly low prices.

Winco's advertising is built around a simple but important concept in marketing: proof. *If you make a claim in your advertising or marketing, you must back it up with proof.*

One ad they use regularly when launching a new store shows a list of typical household items bought from the existing supermarkets in the local area. And here's the kicker - they show the actual receipt from each supermarket, so there's the proof.

This kind of ad is very persuasive, obviously. Of course, if we were cynical we'd point out that they probably selected the featured items carefully to maximize the savings, but that's not the point here. The point is, *proof or even perceived proof works!*

How to Use This Lesson In Your Business

In your business, what kind of proof elements do you incorporate in your marketing? Testimonials for example prove that you have

177

existing happy customers. A photo of your retail store proves that you're an established local company, not a fly by night operator. Sending tracking numbers for packages proves you sent the item.

Most people are naturally skeptical. Therefore, proof is a really important element in marketing, so make sure that you include at least one element of proof in every promotion that you do. If your market is known to be jaded or more skeptical than most, include even more proof!

Chapter 77

Bose

This is another big marketing lesson from Bose. I saw a magazine ad for their 'Quiet Comfort' headphones in the Delta airlines magazine.

At the bottom of the ad was something rather interesting. It said, to order or learn more, there are two options - phone or visit a website. That's straightforward, but with each of those methods of responding, Bose will know exactly how you heard about these headphones.

"How do they do that?" I hear you ask. Well, I shall tell you young Jedi. They include a tracking mechanism.

If you place your order by phone, you're asked to request extension Q7403. Well that doesn't exist as an extension, it's simply a tracking code that tells Bose you read their ad in the Delta magazine. Yes, a secret code - sneaky eh?

For the website address, they don't ask you to go to www.Bose.com, its www.Bose.com/dl (the 'dl' is a code for Delta).

If you visit that link you'll see that it acknowledges that you're a Delta flyer, with the Delta logo at the top of the page.

So why is all of this necessary or important?

Well, Bose probably puts this ad in at least a dozen different airline magazines. If they sent all readers to one phone number, or to www.Bose.com, they'd never know which ad was the most successful. But when they track their marketing with these codes, they can understand exactly which magazines were successful (i.e. profitable), and which were not. And next time they place the ads, they might ditch any magazines that weren't getting good results.

How to Use This Lesson In Your Business

It's important to include tracking mechanisms like those I just mentioned, in your ads. It's vitally important to know exactly which ads are profitable, and which are not - otherwise you're just wasting money.

Chapter 78

Samsung

I noticed in one of the technology magazines that Samsung had released the first cell phone for the Welsh market in the United Kingdom - maybe Tom Jones had put pressure on them?

I found the launch of this new cellphone fascinating because, although I couldn't find an exact number of people that speak Welsh, my research indicated that there's about ¾ of a million welsh speakers in the British Isles, with a further 250,000 in other parts of the world. All together, it's around a million worldwide.

Now a million is not a large number as a niche in the bigger picture of mobile phone users worldwide, but it's still a large demographic of people with money to spend, who didn't have a cell phone in their own language.

Samsung had obviously done extensive research to find this hungry, underserved market and they developed some new software for the operating system, which includes 44,000 welsh words.

The phone is being offered free with a two year contract, and as it's currently a unique offering, a one of a kind for the welsh market, I'm sure that they'll sell a truck load of them. Maybe even two truck loads.

181

How to Use This Lesson In Your Business

The lesson to adapt for your business is to *look out for underserved markets, and offer something for them.*

As I mentioned, Samsung already manufacture and sell mobile phones. They simply tweaked their software to serve a niche market that was desperate to get a phone in their own language.

As another example to illustrate the lesson, think about a photographer. Maybe they're currently photographing weddings at the weekend, but why couldn't they branch out to also do school photos, portraits, sports photography, product shots, concerts, parties, passports, and so on? In each case, they'd be using their core skill as a photographer in other areas that have lots more customers than their current niche.

As another example, think about an electrician. They might have been specializing in domestic work, perhaps installing cables in new homes. They could use the same core skills to install telephone, network, or fire alarm cables. Or they could offer a testing service to check electrical installations for safety. Get the idea? Look for ways to diversify what you do, to serve markets that are hungry for it.

182

Chapter 79

IKEA

This is another big marketing lesson from IKEA. I've featured IKEA in the past for different reasons, but this is another lesson about something I haven't talked about before.

As a reminder, IKEA is a Swedish company that has revolutionized the way that people buy furniture and household items. They have huge warehouses that you wander around, and

when you find something you like, you pick it off the shelf and if it's a furniture item it's usually down to you to assemble it. In other words, most of the items are flat packs, which saves you money.

When you enter an IKEA store you'll see a big poster along with flyers like the one on the left. It's a calendar for the month with something happening on each day.

183

For example, on certain days there are special discounts, on other days you get bonus items with a purchase, and there's even a day where you can get breakfast for free. The point is, they've created physical events around their business - there's always something happening to tempt people back to the store again.

How to Use This Lesson In Your Business

Whether your business is online or offline you should *create a marketing calendar, with daily, weekly, or even monthly specials.* Every business can do that, can't they?

Inject some personality, color, and fun into it, and make the events special.

Apart from anything else, this kind of calendar gives you an excuse to keep in touch with customers and keep your business name in front of them.

Chapter 80

Sport Clips

SportClips is a U.S. based hairdressing chain. This business is a great example of the fact that there's "riches in niches".

These days, if you want your hair cut you can walk into any one of hundreds of thousands of hair salons and to be honest, they'll all look and feel pretty much the same - there's nothing to differentiate one from another.

But that's not the case with SportClips because, as the name suggests, it's a sports themed environment. Know any guys that are into sports? Right, say no more.

Each store revolves around sports, with metal lockers, sports posters, flags, and so on - you can even watch sports while getting your haircut. So by theming what is normally a commodity service, they've managed to carve out a niche slice of the market and build a happy array of loyal customers.

How to Use This Lesson In Your Business

The lesson for your business is that *the closer you can get to matching someone's interests, the more likely they are to do business with you.*

SportClips is a really good example because while most guys don't particularly look forward to going to the hairdresser, if they're interested in sports it suddenly becomes much more appealing; they will have a positive experience which inherently encourages them to go back again and again.

SportClips is also a great example of transforming an inherently boring, commodity type business. Yes, any business can be transformed to make it more appealing.

Chapter 81

Evian

This big marketing lesson is from Evian, the well known water supplier. You can buy bottles of Evian in almost any supermarket, just like many other brands; in fact bottled water is now a competitive industry. But did you know that you can also buy a premium bottle of Evian in some fancy restaurants? It's called the Palace bottle, it costs around $20, and it looks like this:

According to Evian, "It was designed to represent the modern vision of Evian while maintaining a strong tie to our heritage in the French Alps. It's designed to provide a true luxury water experience."

A 'truly luxury water experience', eh? I always thought water was water, but I guess I'm wrong ;)

As if to further prove the point of what you can get away with when marketing water, you can also buy a product called *Evian Facial Spray*. It's a mineral water spray, but this is how the marketing materials sell it:

"Evian's delightful cool mist rehydrates skin suffering from overheated or dry office air. It also revives your makeup throughout the day, and keeps you looking fresh by replenishing that much needed moisture."

It's water!

And it turns out that there's quite a market for it because they've been selling this product for more than thirty years at up to fifteen bucks a pop. The cheaper alternative...to splash yourself while standing at the sink doesn't seem to have the same appeal for some people.

How to Use This Lesson In Your Business

The lesson for your business is that *any product can be premiumized.* I'm not sure if that's even a word, but let's pretend that it is. Yes, *any product can have a high-end, significantly more expensive version.* If they can do it with water, then you can do it with your products and services, regardless of what they are. No excuses! I don't want to hear "but Andrew, my business is different!" If you can create premium water, then you can create premium *anything*.

Remember, in any market there are always about 20% of buyers that just want the best you have to offer. It really doesn't matter what it is. If there's a more expensive option, they'll take it.

Think about that for your business. What could you offer that's a higher end alternative for those customers that want the best?

Obviously if you don't offer a premium version then they're not going to buy it, but if it's available, some of them will. So make it available! Let me remind you that Evian spelled backwards is naive! Hmmm, a thought to ponder on!

Chapter 82

XM Sirius Satellite Radio

This big marketing lesson is from XM Satellite Radio. Now, the last time I bought a new car, it came with a three-month trial of the XM service. So I took advantage of the offer and took it for a test drive (no pun intended...or maybe it was).

After about a month, I received a letter from XM that said something along the lines of "we'd like to charge you now if that's okay". Well actually XM, it's not okay. Why? Because I tried the service and it was horrible. The quality of the music was like listening through a tin can and a long piece of string. Apparently, they've compressed the signal so much that to call it low fidelity would be a compliment.

It's ironic that you have this much hyped, groundbreaking innovation of satellite radio, but the quality is a giant leap backwards, much worse than FM in my opinion. If you're a techy person it's my understanding that the average bit rate of XM is 64kb per second. To put that into perspective, most MP3 recordings use a minimum of 128kbps (twice the bit rate), and even that's not classed as high fidelity.

Okay, so enough of the rant, what's the lesson here? Well, frankly, XM's three month trial offer and the subsequent letter they sent me were all pointless because they fell at the first hurdle - in my opinion they had a crappy product! *The quality of the products and services you sell must stand out from the crowd of alternative options.*

How to Use This Lesson In Your Business

In your business, how often do you closely consider the quality of your products? It's really important, because ultimately no amount of creative marketing can make up for a terrible product. And besides, why would you want to inflict a bad product on the world? It's not that difficult to make something great.

In the case of XM, as I understand it, they could reduce the number of channels, which would enable them to equal or surpass CD quality. If they did that, I'd subscribe in a heartbeat, but for now, XM continues to lose subscribers because the sound quality is so poor.

Chapter 83

Disney Movies

You may have noticed that that Disney only offers their older movies for a limited time. You'll typically see an ad that says something like this one:

"Beat the Vault - Pickup these timeless Disney classics before they go into the vault."

Of course there is no vault, but it sounds a lot better than saying we're taking them off the shelves and putting them back into a big dusty warehouse in New Jersey.

As a very real example of this, at the time I was researching this book, you were no longer be able to buy the movies 101 Dalmatians, Cars, Finding Nemo, and Mary Poppins among others. They'd been put 'back in the vault', so to speak.

This is a marketing principle called *'scarcity', which means limiting some aspect of the sale.* I've referred to it previously, in the example of the Nintendo Wii. Remember that one?

In the Disney example, they limit the *time* that the DVD's are available, but scarcity can apply to other elements, too. For example, you might have a limited *number* of units available, or you might offer free installation to the first x many customers only.

Basically, scarcity is designed to encourage buyers to avoid procrastinating. As marketers, we want people to decide *now* to make a purchase, because if they leave it until later, chances are they'll forget or change their mind, and ultimately they won't buy at that later date. That sucks for us, especially after we've worked so hard to make the sale!

It's worth mentioning that scarcity, despite the sound of that word, shouldn't involve being scary. It should be positioned as a positive benefit of acting fast; it should never involve intimidation or high pressure selling.

Remember to give a *valid reason* for the scarcity. For example, if you're offering a document that can be downloaded, it makes no sense to say "we only have 300 available" because it's digital, and there's no practical limit with delivering that document. In that example, we might say, "this information is so valuable that I'm limiting it to the first 300 people who respond". See the difference? It's subtle, but important, if you want to have credibility.

How to Use This Lesson In Your Business

What elements of your products or services could you place a perceived limit on, in order to encourage buyers not to procrastinate? Let me know if you've seen any good examples of scarcity in other people's marketing by sending me an email to: andrew@helpmybusiness.com.

Chapter 84

data robotics, inc.™

Data Robotics

This big marketing lesson is from Data robotics, makers of the innovative Drobo product, which backs up computer data safely on multiple hard disks, for extra protection.

I saw an ad for the Drobo and although it's a good ad, there's a very specific reason that I wanted to highlight it for you – the placement of the ad. In other words, the media it appeared in, and why.

The ad appeared in the magazine *Photoshop User,* which targets digital artists who use the software Adobe Photoshop.

The marketing principle involved is what my friend Dan Kennedy calls "message to market match". I couldn't come up with a better name for it, so he deserves credit for naming the concept. "Message to market match" means, in essence, *putting your marketing message in front of the audience who are most likely to respond.*

In the Drobo example, the message is:

"With the New Drobo S, Protecting Your Priceless Photographs is Simple."

That's the message, so who do you think is the best market for that message? Well, surely its people who work with photographs, right? Right!

So now let's look at where the ad appeared again, *Photoshop User* Magazine. So this is an excellent example of "message to market match". *Every* reader of this magazine is a potential customer for the Drobo!

This marketing principle may sounds obvious to you, but you wouldn't believe how many businesses mess this up.

Consider an example...

Suppose that you're a Seattle based supplier of chicken and steak products to restaurants all over the western U.S. You've got great products, great customer service, and restaurant owners that have tried your products love them. It's a perfect match, right? Well, if you were to send out a marketing piece or ad to restaurants in the Seattle area, your response might be poor, at best. I guarantee it. Why? Because Seattle has one of the largest concentrations of vegetarian restaurants in the U.S! Can you see the point here?!

You could send out the most persuasive marketing every day to those vegetarian restaurants, but they're never going to buy your meat products because they're simply not a match for your message or offer.

How to Use This Lesson In Your Business

In your business, think about who your ideal customer is, and think carefully, because as the example I just gave you proves - your customer is NOT everyone. It's always a *specific* group of people.

Once you know who your ideal customers are, the next job is to find out where they are. Where do they hang out, whether online or offline? Once you identify the *where*, you then have a message to market match.

This marketing principle is a fundamental of effective marketing, so much so that I can confidently say, whenever you have a marketing campaign that's ineffective, it's highly likely that you *didn't* have a good message to market match.

Chapter 85

Nielsen

You probably know Nielsen as a research company; they've been around for many years and somehow I made it on to one of their lists because I received a plain looking envelope from them that I almost threw away. I don't know about you, but I sort my mail over the bin, the garbage can, and anything that looks like junk mail gets thrown away without even being opened. Do you do that? I bet you do!

Anyway, I opened the envelope and to my surprise, it included a request to fill out a brief survey along with five $1 bills!

Real money grabs your attention, doesn't it?! I would have normally thrown this kind of survey away, but because there was money included in the envelope, the guilt I felt compelled me to complete and return it.

My reaction incidentally, is very typical. Most people react in the same way, and that's because there's a psychological rule working behind the scenes, called 'reciprocity'.

I first learned about it in the book *Influence: The Psychology of Persuasion*. In that book, author Robert Cialdini shares his discovery that *when someone does something nice for us, we feel absolutely compelled to reciprocate.* We just can't help ourselves, it happens subconsciously, without us realizing it. So it's a fascinating principle when applied to marketing, because in this example with Nielsen, it definitely worked.

Even though the five one-dollar bills couldn't possibly equate to the value of my time to fill out the survey, I did, because of the rule of reciprocity. Interesting, isn't it?

Now, despite leveraging the rule of reciprocity, there was still a fundamental flaw in this marketing piece.

You might remember that I said that I almost didn't open the envelope because it looked like junk mail. So, here's a question for you. What message could they have put on the envelope to make me open it? Obviously they can't put 'get your $5 cash inside' or anything like that, because we all know that the envelope wouldn't have ever made it to me. But can you think of anything else that they could have put in there?

Think about that, you can also review the comments that others made in the archives when this episode was first released at www.HelpMyBusiness.com, and you can email me your thoughts at: andrew@helpmynbusiness.com

How to Use This Lesson In Your Business

Incentives can work effectively, but you must think them through before rolling out a marketing campaign. Put yourself in the shoes of the prospect receiving your marketing piece.

Chapter 86

Soundview Executive Book Summaries

This big marketing lesson is from Soundview Executive Book Summaries.

Soundview offers a simple concept, and it's explained very well on their website.

On the left hand side we see:

'Problem: Sssssso many great business books, so little time'.

On the right hand side we see:

'Solution: Soundview executive book summaries'.

This approach to advertising - to state the problem and solution - is as old as dirt, but it works. In fact, it really is a proven formula for effective advertising. First, state a problem that the audience relates to. Then offer a solution. Sounds obvious, doesn't it? But, the fact is many business owners focus on *prevention* rather than solution, and prevention is very hard to sell.

199

To take an example, if a computer nerd offers a service to help people prevent a virus on their computer, that's a tough product to sell because the target audience isn't feeling any pain. They know that they may or may not get a virus, but as it stands things are good, so they'll probably procrastinate.

On the other hand, if the computer nerd offers to eliminate any virus within 30 minutes or less, now that's a very appealing offer. The computer user who *has* a virus is feeling a lot of pain. They might be losing files; they may not even be able to start the computer. If you've had that situation, you know that you're chomping at the bit to get a solution fast, and price virtually becomes irrelevant.

Hopefully, you're convinced that it's much better it is to offer a solution rather than a prevention. And coming back to the ad from Soundview, it's an excellent example of that model. We all know that there are too many business books to get through, and we don't want to miss out on the great advice and tips that they contain, so Soundview Summaries are a convenient solution.

How to Use This Lesson In Your Business

Take another look at how you're positioning your products and services, particularly in advertising. ***Are you offering prevention or solution?*** If it's prevention, see if there's a way to change the positioning, to move it to a solution oriented offer.

200

Chapter 87

Arby's

This big marketing lesson is from Arby's, the fast food chain. On a recent visit, the receipt had a message on the front that I couldn't miss. It said:

Free roast beef sandwich

Not being one to pass up a freebie, I took a closer look. On the back of the receipt, this offer was clearly stated:

Free regular roast beef or beef 'n' cheddar, call or visit the website and complete a survey.

Now, a lot of retail outlets invite customers to complete a survey, but most of them don't offer any incentive for the customer to do that. Frankly, that's just plain stupid.

Basic human psychology says that when you give someone an incentive, they're much more likely to take action. Filling out a survey isn't exactly most people's idea of fun, but they'll probably do it if you dangle a nice carrot in front of them. Or, in this case, a roast beef sandwich.

How to Use This Lesson In Your Business

Avoid the assumption that customers will take an action you want them to take. Use incentives, because they work.

Note that the incentive doesn't have to be anything earth-shattering; it can actually be quite modest. But offer something that has mass appeal.

The other lesson here is to make a big deal about the incentive. Arby's did a good job with plastering the offer on the front and back of the receipt. You can't miss it. Arby's knows that if you look at the receipt, you'll at least consider the offer.

The other hidden benefit of this type of offer is that the cost of doing the survey is next to nothing. Why? Because the customer has to go back to the store to redeem their free sandwich. And let's face it, how many people will *only* order a sandwich? That's very unlikely. It's much more likely that the customer will end up buying all kinds of extra items. That's the law of averages, and it can be counted on.

So this is smart marketing. You can acquire valuable feedback at zero cost using this kind of offer on the customer receipt.

Chapter 88

Bud Light Beer

Annheuser Busch, the makers of Budweiser Light Beer, put out a commercial which you may or may not have seen. It was a parody of the popular TV show "Lost", with a unique twist to promote the beer.

I really liked the commercial. I thought it was well done; it instantly looked like "Lost" and it had some good humor. But what's the big marketing lesson here?

It's the fact that this commercial was timed to coincide with a significant event that was on a lot of people's minds - the final season of the TV show *Lost*! There was a lot of buzz around the show; people were wondering how the plot was going to develop, what would happen with the characters, and so on.

The lesson for us is that *tying in with topical news or current events is a very good marketing strategy.* It makes it very easy for people to pass on the message, which is what every business wants. Word of mouth recommendation is the ultimate marketing goal.

So how can you adapt this principle in your business? Well, I'll let you in on a secret. Marketing that ties in with news and current events doesn't happen by accident or luck. Actually, let me clarify. *Sometimes* all the pieces of the puzzle happen to all drop into place at the same time to make for a freak, opportunistic circumstance, but it's rare.

Marketing opportunities like this are commonly planned far in advance. In this example with Bud Light, the creators of the commercial would have planned it many months before the new season of Lost was due to air. That kind of planning makes for a well thought out, and effective campaign.

How to Use This Lesson In Your Business

Be on the lookout for marketing opportunities that will happen in the future. There are lots of events that can create great tie-ins for you. For example, what about an upcoming election? Or how about entertainment industry events like the Grammy's, Oscar's, or Golden Globes? They always get air-time, so you can piggyback on their popularity, by planning ahead. Planning is the key to success. To summarize, *look out for opportunities to tie your marketing message into something that's already popular, or you know will be popular in the future.*

204

Chapter 89

Heinz

One of the best selling products for Heinz is...can you guess? It's ketchup. Obviously, it's an enormous seller and the brand leader by a mile. But Heinz didn't rest on their laurels...

They conducted a study some years ago where they sent a team of researchers into people's homes, to watch how they used ketchup. I'm sure they saw all kinds of perfectly tasty food wrecked by engulfing it in an avalanche of ketchup, but that's beside the point.

As it turns out, they discovered something that they previously had no idea about. It turns out that young children like to pour ketchup themselves, but the heavy glass bottles combined with their feeble attempts to bash the base, meant that most kids couldn't get more than a micro dollop on their plate. Can you see where this is heading?

Armed with that research, Heinz went back to the lab and came up with a brand new squeezable plastic bottle that's very easy to use, even by kids.

As a result of that innovation, and the fact that kids began to pour more ketchup onto their plates, sales went up by 12 percent! Now that might not sound like much, but a 12 percent rise in a competitive market where you're already the leader, is enormous.

It accounts for many millions of dollars in additional revenue every year.

How to Use This Lesson In Your Business

The lesson here is to study how your customers use your products or services, and try and make improvements accordingly.

Even if you're the market leader like Heinz, their example proves that they still had room for improvement.

So wherever you're at in your business, take time to study your customers and learn from them. On the simplest level, survey them, but ideally interact with them, walk in their shoes, observe what they do with your product. You'll be amazed at what you discover.

Chapter 90

The Cheesecake Factory

This big marketing lesson is from the Cheesecake Factory, a U.S. based restaurant chain that has an outstanding reputation for quality food and great service.

Luci and I were enjoying a meal at our local Cheesecake Factory in Salt Lake City, and I had asked for warm chicken on my salad, but when it came out, the chicken was chilled. It wasn't a big deal, I didn't throw a fit or anything, but when I mentioned it to the server, he immediately offered to resolve the issue, and he also happily comped us a free dessert too.

By contrast, we were at another restaurant chain a week later and when Luci's steak came out, it wasn't what she'd ordered. The server barely apologized, and basically hoped that we'd just overlook it. Bizarre. What a contrast with Cheesecake Factory, who Luci and I both enthusiastically recommend to other people, despite the fact that they make mistakes.

Actually, let's be clear about this. Every company makes mistakes, frequently. There isn't a business on the planet that doesn't screw up regularly; it's just a fact of life. *What matters is how the mistakes are handled and rectified.*

207

How to Use This Lesson In Your Business

The lesson for your business is, first of all, ***have a set of pre-determined service standards in place***, reflecting a specific commitment to your customers.

In an ideal world, what do you want customers to experience when they interact with your business? Once you know what that looks like, decide in advance how you'll handle situations when your customer service fails to match up to your own standards.

Can you see the point here? Most companies either don't care about customer service, or they do, but it's handled inconsistently because there's no system for it. One employee might do a good job of keeping a customer happy, whereas another might damage a relationship, perhaps permanently. So it's a serious issue.

You must have a system in place for customer service, and train employees how to handle each type of issue that comes up.

Chapter 91

MOLESKINE®
Legendary notebooks

Moleskine Notebooks

Here's an example of a Moleskine notebook that a friend sent me:

So how do you sell a product as plain as a notebook? I mean, come on, it's just pieces of paper bound together, isn't it? Well, if you're Moleskine, you craft a compelling story, transforming the product into something compelling. Here, let me share with you an example of how they do it. Here's the opening paragraph from their promotional blurb. It says:

"Moleskine is the legendary notebook used by European artists and thinkers for the past two centuries, from Van Gogh to Picasso, from Ernest Hemingway to Bruce Chatwin. This trusty, pocket size travel companion held sketches, notes, stories and ideas before they were turned into famous images or pages of beloved books."

209

And it then goes onto describe the origin of the notebook in Parisian stationery shops. The story paints quite a picture, in fact it's compelling reading.

Can you see how your perception of a simple notebook can be quickly transformed? Already, we're closer to believing that if we use this notebook, it'll have some kind of magical power to transform us into the next DaVinci! Its classic marketing, isn't it?

How to Use This Lesson In Your Business

This is a good reminder that ***even the most mundane, boring products can be transformed into something desirable, with creative, well thought out marketing.*** I hope this example inspires you to create some new, persuasive copy for your products or services.

Chapter 92

Concluding Comments and an Irresistible Offer

Congratulations! By making it this far you already know more about effective marketing than most business owners.

What happens now?

Honestly, in a book like this it is impossible to reveal every little tip, technique, and secret, because marketing is such a large, ever changing subject.

I'm sure you realize that it makes sense to keep up to date with the latest information and discoveries.

My Free Gift to You

The real gift is not a ring box with a bow on it, it's better than that

I'm happy to tell you that I've put together a special video series that explains some additional powerful marketing strategies that aren't contained in this book. They're free, and they're incredibly useful. They're my way of expressing thanks to you, for investing your time and money in buying and reading this book.

I've conservatively put a value of $175 on these videos, and **you can receive them absolutely free by simply following the instructions below:**

How to Get the FREE Video Training, valued at $175:

Visit: www.SendMyFreeGift.com

You'll get instant access to the videos online.

Take Action!

I honestly believe that this book has a true value of at least one hundred times the cover price. Please don't mistake that as arrogance. I'll explain...

I'm convinced that any serious student of marketing, with a great product or service, can run with the information in these pages to build a business where they would easily surpass one hundred times the cost of this book in a relatively short time, by implementing just a few of the strategies contained in these pages.

Again, congratulations for discovering these unconventional marketing methods that were born at some of the biggest brands in the world. I look forward to hearing your success story.